T0328963

CAMBRIDGE LIBRARY COLLECTION

Books of enduring scholarly value

Archaeology

The discovery of material remains from the recent or the ancient past has always been a source of fascination, but the development of archaeology as an academic discipline which interpreted such finds is relatively recent. It was the work of Winckelmann at Pompeii in the 1760s which first revealed the potential of systematic excavation to scholars and the wider public. Pioneering figures of the nineteenth century such as Schliemann, Layard and Petrie transformed archaeology from a search for ancient artifacts, by means as crude as using gunpowder to break into a tomb, to a science which drew from a wide range of disciplines - ancient languages and literature, geology, chemistry, social history - to increase our understanding of human life and society in the remote past.

The Holy Sepulchre and the Temple at Jerusalem

Born in Scotland, James Fergusson (1808–86) spent ten years as an indigo planter in India before embarking upon a second career as an architectural historian. Despite his lack of formal training, he became an expert in the field of Indian architecture. The topography and temples of ancient Jerusalem also fascinated him. This 1865 collection of two lectures summarises his controversial topographical and architectural argument that the location where Constantine erected the original Holy Sepulchre was the Dome of the Rock on the Temple Mount. Fergusson then describes the Temple in its successive forms, arguing against the view that the rock known as the foundation stone was the site of the Jewish altar. The work is illustrated throughout with plans and drawings. Fergusson's *Cave Temples of India* (1880) and the two-volume revised edition of his *History of Indian and Eastern Architecture* (1910) are also reissued in the Cambridge Library Collection.

Cambridge University Press has long been a pioneer in the reissuing of out-of-print titles from its own backlist, producing digital reprints of books that are still sought after by scholars and students but could not be reprinted economically using traditional technology. The Cambridge Library Collection extends this activity to a wider range of books which are still of importance to researchers and professionals, either for the source material they contain, or as landmarks in the history of their academic discipline.

Drawing from the world-renowned collections in the Cambridge University Library and other partner libraries, and guided by the advice of experts in each subject area, Cambridge University Press is using state-of-the-art scanning machines in its own Printing House to capture the content of each book selected for inclusion. The files are processed to give a consistently clear, crisp image, and the books finished to the high quality standard for which the Press is recognised around the world. The latest print-on-demand technology ensures that the books will remain available indefinitely, and that orders for single or multiple copies can quickly be supplied.

The Cambridge Library Collection brings back to life books of enduring scholarly value (including out-of-copyright works originally issued by other publishers) across a wide range of disciplines in the humanities and social sciences and in science and technology.

The Holy Sepulchre
and the Temple at Jerusalem

*Being the Substance of Two Lectures,
Delivered in the Royal Institution*

JAMES FERGUSSON

CAMBRIDGE
UNIVERSITY PRESS

CAMBRIDGE
UNIVERSITY PRESS

University Printing House, Cambridge, CB2 8BS, United Kingdom

Cambridge University Press is part of the University of Cambridge.
It furthers the University's mission by disseminating knowledge in the pursuit of
education, learning and research at the highest international levels of excellence.

www.cambridge.org
Information on this title: www.cambridge.org/9781108080637

This edition first published 1865
This digitally printed version 2015

ISBN 978-1-108-08063-7 Paperback

This book reproduces the text of the original edition. The content and language reflect
the beliefs, practices and terminology of their time, and have not been updated.

VIEW OF THE TEMPLE AS IT APPEARED AT THE TIME OF THE CRUCIFIXION.

THE

HOLY SEPULCHRE

AND THE

TEMPLE AT JERUSALEM.

BEING THE SUBSTANCE OF TWO LECTURES DELIVERED IN THE
ROYAL INSTITUTION, ALBEMARLE STREET, ON THE
21st FEBRUARY, 1862, AND 3rd MARCH, 1865.

By JAMES FERGUSSON, F.R.S.,

FELLOW OF THE ROYAL INST. BRIT. ARCH.;

AUTHOR OF ' AN ESSAY ON THE ANCIENT TOPOGRAPHY OF JERUSALEM,' ETC. ETC.

Golden Gateway. From a Photograph.

LONDON:

JOHN MURRAY, ALBEMARLE STREET.

1865.

The right of Translation is reserved.

Works by the same Author.

AN ESSAY ON THE ANCIENT TOPOGRAPHY OF JERUSA-
LEM; with restored Plans of the Temple, and with Plans, Sections, and Details of
the Church built by Constantine the Great over the Holy Sepulchre, now known as
the Mosque of Omar. 16s., or 21s. half Russia. London, Weale, 1847.

THE ILLUSTRATED HANDBOOK OF ARCHITECTURE. Being
a Concise and Popular Account of the Different Styles prevailing in all Ages and
all Countries. With 850 Illustrations. 8vo. 26s. London, Murray, 1859.

HISTORY OF THE MODERN STYLES OF ARCHITECTURE.
Being a Sequel to the 'Handbook of Architecture.' With 312 Illustrations. 8vo.
31s. 6d London, Murray, 1862.

AN HISTORICAL INQUIRY INTO THE TRUE PRINCIPLES OF
BEAUTY IN ART, more especially with reference to Architecture. Royal 8vo.
31s. 6d. London, Longmans, 1849.

THE PALACES OF NINEVEH AND PERSEPOLIS RESTORED :
An Essay on Ancient Assyrian and Persian Architecture. 8vo. 16s. London,
Murray, 1851.

ILLUSTRATIONS OF THE ROCK-CUT TEMPLES OF INDIA.
18 Plates in Tinted Lithography, folio : with an 8vo. volume of Text, Plans, &c.
2l. 7s. 6d. London, Weale, 1845.

PICTURESQUE ILLUSTRATIONS OF ANCIENT ARCHITEC-
TURE IN HINDOSTAN. 24 Plates in coloured Lithography, with Plans, Woodcuts, and explanatory Text, &c. 4l. 4s. London, Hogarth, 1847.

AN ESSAY ON A PROPOSED NEW SYSTEM OF FORTIFICA-
TION, with Hints for its Application to our National Defences. 12s. 6d. London,
Weale, 1849.

THE PERIL OF PORTSMOUTH. FRENCH FLEETS AND ENGLISH
FORTS. Plan. 8vo. 3s. London, Murray, 1853.

PORTSMOUTH PROTECTED : with Notes on Sebastopol and other
Sieges during the Present War. Plans. 8vo. 3s. London, Murray, 1856.

OBSERVATIONS ON THE BRITISH MUSEUM, NATIONAL
GALLERY, and NATIONAL RECORD OFFICE; with Suggestions for their
Improvement. 8vo. London, Weale, 1859.

NOTES ON THE SITE OF THE HOLY SEPULCHRE AT JERU-
SALEM. An answer to 'The Edinburgh Review.' 2s. 6d. London, Murray, 1861.

THE MAUSOLEUM AT HALICARNASSUS RESTORED, IN CON-
FORMITY WITH THE REMAINS RECENTLY DISCOVERED. Plates. 4to. 7s. 6d. London, Murray, 1862.

LONDON : PRINTED BY W. CLOWES AND SONS, STAMFORD-STREET, AND CHARING-CROSS.

PREFACE.

DURING the eighteen years that have elapsed since the publication of the 'Essay on the Ancient Topography of Jerusalem,' a considerable amount of accurate information has been collected, bearing on the questions therein discussed. This would be sufficient, under ordinary circumstances, to justify a second edition of the work; but there are several reasons why this should hardly yet be attempted.

First—There is a survey now in progress at Jerusalem, which will rectify our knowledge of the topography to a very considerable extent, but, though completed on the spot, it will not be published and available to the public for some time to come.

Secondly—The works of De Vogüé and De Saulcy are still incomplete, and will no doubt throw important light on many points of interest; and there are other researches in progress which have a more or less direct bearing on the points at issue.

The most important reason, however, for deferring the second edition is, that the questions raised on the original work have not yet reached that stage which entitles them to the consideration of earnest and competent inquirers.

When a question of this kind is first brought forward, it meets only with contempt, and sneers supply the place of arguments. When these will no longer suffice, misrepresentation of the facts of the case, and abuse of the author who brought it forward, serve to keep back the truth for some time. If it survives these, it is then taken up by those who ought to have investigated it when first promulgated, and what is good in it established, what is erroneous put on one side.

My own impression is, that the theory, that the Dome of the Rock was built by Constantine, has passed through the first two of these stages of its existence; but whether it has reached the third is by no means so clear. It is so much easier to criticise than to investigate; so much safer to deny than to admit an hypothesis which may afterwards be proved to be untenable; so much pleasanter to detect another in error, than to acknowledge his success even in the slightest degree, that from one or all of these causes the great difficulty of such a case as this, is to obtain for it a fair hearing.

It would have been as easy to point out any flaw in arguments adduced eighteen years ago, as it may be now. The facts and the arguments were so simple and so broadly stated, that the refutation, if it could be made, must have been distinct and crushing ; but it has not yet been brought forward. The question therefore remains exactly where it was eighteen years ago, except in this respect—if I am not mistaken—that it is now attracting a certain amount of public attention; and if so, unless the heresy can be up-rooted, it will inevitably come to be accepted in the course of time.

Under these circumstances, it appears expedient to lay before the public a short and compendious statement of the case, in order that those who wish for information may obtain it in the clearest manner, and with the least amount of trouble to themselves, and may be enabled to judge how far the arguments generally employed to disprove it really meet the merits of the case.

For these purposes, it has been determined to print two Lectures on the subject, which were delivered at the Royal Institution in Albemarle Street—one in February 1862, the other in March last. These do not, of course, pretend to be exhaustive statements of the case; but they do con-tain a *résumé* of all the main points of the argument, with a sufficient amount of illustration and references to make it intelligible.

Those who wish for further information are referred to the 'Essay on the Topography of Jerusalem,' above referred to; to the articles 'Jerusalem' and 'Temple,' in Smith's 'Dictionary of the Bible ;' and to the 'Notes on the Site of the Holy Sepulchre,' published in 1861, in answer to an attack in the 'Edinburgh Review.'

These may be considered as the pleadings on one side of the question, but it need hardly be added that they do not suffice to enable any one to form an independent opinion on the subject, unless he is also familiar with what has been written on the opposite side. Even after mastering these, no one is properly entitled to judge who has not had previous education in matters of this sort, and unless he is prepared to study the original authorities, and to investigate the topographical details for himself. All this may require more leisure and more enthusiasm than most people are willing to devote to such a subject. If they try, however, they will probably find it intensely interesting, and, if I am not mistaken, worthy of all the pains that can be bestowed upon it even by the first class of minds.

Whenever it is so investigated, I have no fears of the result; until it is so taken up, it is only a waste of time and temper to attempt to struggle against the indifference of many, and the special pleading of those who cling to a tradition which has no logical basis to rest upon.

Since this work was in the press, a small volume has been received from abroad, entitled 'Theodericus de Locis Sanctis,' with appendices, edited by the well-known Dr. Titus Tobler, of St. Gall, one of the most stanch supporters of the present traditional Sepulchre of Jerusalem. Though too late to admit of all the use being made of it which might have been done had it been received earlier, the principal

passages bearing on the argument have been reprinted
at length in the Appendix to this work.

The first extract from the description of an anonymous
traveller* settles the long-disputed question of the site
of the Porta Neapolitana. This was the only historical
difficulty that really existed, which, though not important
in itself, was still sufficiently so to render its removal satisfactory. The second,† giving the inscriptions on the
Dome of the Rock, as they existed A.D. 1172, renders it
nearly certain that the Arabic inscriptions which now adorn
that building are as late as Saladin's time, as suggested in
the text; and the reiterated assertion of Theodericus that
that building was erected by Constantine and his mother
Helena, as Dr. Tobler says, "takes the blush of novelty off
Mr. Fergusson's theory," though in a manner which may be
considered most satisfactory.

A third extract, quoted below,‡ is as important as either of
these, and would be more so if the indication of the locality
were a little more precise. As it stands, it proves, however,
that the "lapis pertusus" of the Bordeaux Pilgrim and the
Innominatus (Appendices A and B) still existed in his
day, and that it stood within the limits of the Temple, as
determined in the second Lecture contained in this volume.§

---

* Appendix B.

† Appendix D.

‡ Inter templum quoque et duo la-
tera atrii exterioris, orientale scilicet et
meridianum *lapis magnus situs est
in modum altaris* qui secundum quo-
rundam traditiones, os est piscinarum
ibidem consistentium, secundum alio-
rum vero opinionem Zachariam Bara-
chiæ filium ibidem peremtum fuisse
designat (p. 37).

§ The interior court of the text is

The tradition, that it covered the entrance of the great cistern, is sufficient to prove that it stood in front of the Aksah, though whether on the exact spot where the Jewish altar once stood, is not clear, neither is it important, because it certainly was not the altar itself, and whatever it originally represented may have been moved from its original locality.

The circumstance which renders the knowledge of the existence of this stone in the 12th century of importance to our present inquiry, is the fact that it almost certainly was the Sakhra of Mahometan historians; although here again the vagueness that attaches to some of their traditions as we now possess them, detracts somewhat from the precision of their indications.

The stone which the Jews in the 4th century annually repaired to, to anoint and weep over, the Christians in the 5th and 6th centuries had covered with a dunghill, in order to show their contempt of the hated race. In the 7th century this filth was removed by the Moslems, and the stone again restored to honour; and Omar built his mosque immediately behind it, as related in the text (pp. 51 and 105). It is not to be wondered at, that, in the Christian times of Theodericus, the tradition regarding it should again have become as indistinct as that regarding the origin of the Mosque el Aksah itself; but its existence at all is sufficient for our present purposes. It is a direct testimony that the Sakhra which Omar crept through the Gate of Mohammed

the platform on which the Dome of the Rock now stands; the *exterior* court, the remainder of the Haram Area which surrounded it.

on his hands and knees to look for, was not the Sakhra under the Dome of the Rock, but this Lapis Magnus of Theodericus, which still may exist, and perhaps may still be found when looked for.

There is yet another indication in the passage printed in Appendix D, from this work, which is nearly as important in fixing the true site of the sacred localities.

After completing his description of the Dome of the Rock, Theodericus next describes the circular chapel containing the Tomb of St. James, which stood where the Dome of the Chain now stands, within twenty feet of the eastern entrance of the so-called Mosque of Omar. Even if we assume this to be a mere legend, it seems impossible that such a tradition could have existed if there had been a suspicion that the Dome of the Rock was built by the Mahometans, or that it stood within the Temple precincts. Indeed, it does not seem possible to account for the juxta-position, except on the supposition that those who erected it desired that the sepulchre of St. James should be in the closest possible proximity to that of Him who, in the text, is called his brother.

Taken altogether, this little volume is by far the most valuable contribution to the history of the Holy Places which has been made of late years; and it is extremely creditable to the candour of its editor that he should have published a work which tells so seriously against the views he so long and consistently maintained.

The publication of this little work has done so much to

remove the disputed questions regarding the topography of
Jerusalem beyond the limits of discussion, that it is to be
hoped that, if any more such treatises exist in manuscript,
they will before long be given to the world. The real
difficulty of this inquiry hitherto has been, not that the
authorities usually quoted contained anything opposed to
the views I have been advocating, but that the written
evidence was so fragmentary, and frequently so ambiguously
expressed, that it could not be considered as conclusive.
So long, therefore, as those who wrote on the subject insisted
on resting the whole case on the *litera scripta* as it has
hitherto existed, the controversy was, and might for ever
have remained, incapable of final adjustment.

The architectural argument was clear, distinct, and irre-
fragable, and ought to have been considered final, but few
of those who have taken up the question are capable of
expressing an opinion on such evidence, having no such
knowledge of the art as would justify their judgment from
it alone.

The topographical argument was equally clear, and ought
to be considered equally decisive; but this again required
great local knowledge, and more familiarity with details than
can be acquired without a great amount of study, and better
opportunities than are always easily obtainable.

The written argument, on the contrary, is accessible to
any scholar of moderate attainments; consequently nine
out of ten at least, it might almost be said ninety-nine out
of a hundred, of those who have taken up this question,

have been inclined to rest the whole argument on this, which, in this peculiar case, is, and must always be, practically, the least valuable branch of the evidence.

As this state of affairs will probably continue some time longer, it makes the publication of such a work as that of Theodericus most opportune. It is the only really careful and detailed description we have of Jerusalem during the first Latin kingdom. Sæwulf was an ignorant savage, who believed whatever he was told, and was incapable of forming an independent judgment; and Benjamin of Tudela was a credulous Jew, much more interested in legends pertaining to his own race than in general questions of topography. So that Arculfus and Theodericus are the two authorities on which the literary part of the argument must be based in future, and the latter, though only now available, is nearly as important as the former. It cannot, however, be too often repeated that the literary branch of the argument is, from the nature of the case, necessarily the most indistinct, and therefore the least valuable. The architectural evidence is the clearest and most direct, and consequently the most important. The topographical proof ranges next to the architectural. Till these two are disposed of, the historical argument may safely be put aside to wait for further elucidation.

CONTENTS.

———◦◦———

LIST OF ILLUSTRATIONS.

LECTURE

PART I.

INTRODUCTORY.

LADIES AND GENTLEMEN,

I cannot feel that any apology is required for intro-
ducing to your notice a subject which must be to all
Christians the most interesting point of topographical
Archæology. Nor will the place in which I bring it forward
be considered inappropriate, inasmuch as no fortuitous discovery, no mere literary process, but one of pure induc-
tion, such as you continually hear applied in this room
to physical phenomena, has led me from known facts to
legitimate conclusions.

Although, some time since, Archæology was hardly
looked upon as a science, the progress which it has made
during the last few years, the number of facts patiently
observed and carefully recorded, have fully entitled it to
rank among the highest, as it is certainly one of the most
interesting branches of human knowledge.

What I do feel may require some apology to many of you
is, that, in order to make myself perfectly understood by all, I
must begin at the very beginning of my subject, and commence
by telling many of you what you already know as well as I

B

do myself. Without this, I fear some may fail to appreciate
the form of the superstructure from a want of knowledge of
the base on which it is erected.

First, then, you are all of you aware that there is at Jerusalem a famous church known as the Church of the Holy
Sepulchre, situated in the middle of the town, in what is now
known and seems always to have been designated as the
Christian quarter of the Holy City. In its present form this

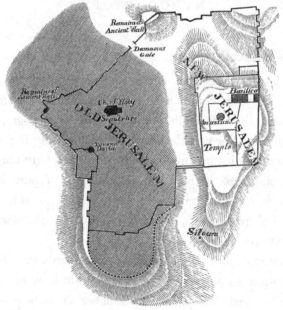

[No. 1.]

church is admitted to have been erected by the Crusaders
during the course of the 12th century, say from A.D. 1100
to 1168. But it is generally believed to have been erected
on the site of the church built at Jerusalem by Constantine
in the 4th century, notwithstanding that no trace of the
previous church is to be found in the present edifice.

Although this is generally—it may almost be said universally—believed, still, on the other hand, many learned
and pious men have entertained grave and serious doubts
as to whether the little tabernacle which occupies the centre
of the Rotunda of this church really does contain the tomb
in which the Saviour was laid—whether, indeed, Constantine
was not entirely mistaken in selecting this position for his
church, and misled by the want of any satisfactory tradition
as to the localities of the scenes of the Passion.

The first person who put these doubts into a tangible form
was a German of the name of Korte, who made a pilgrimage
to Jerusalem about the middle of the last century. When
there he was so struck with what appeared to him the impos-
sibility of reconciling the modern locality with the exigencies
of the Bible narrative, that on his return home he published
a work in which he stated his reasons for doubting whether
what was shown him was or could be the Sepulchre of
Christ. Like most men who announce new and disagreeable
truths, he met only with contempt and contumely, and his
book made no impression on the public. Next to him in
importance, if not in date, was the celebrated Dr. Clarke, of
Cambridge. He visited Jerusalem at the beginning of this
century, and was so struck with the improbability of the supposed site being the true one, that he hardly condescended
to argue the question, and treated it as simply preposterous.

Since his time many sincere and learned men, on visiting
the place, have followed in the same path, and have expressed their doubts in arguments of more or less cogency.
On the other hand, perhaps as many equally sincere and
learned pilgrims have upheld the authenticity of the present
site, and with at least equal success, as they have had all

the *vis inertiæ* of long-established tradition on their side to
supply any failure of logic in dealing with the facts of the
case.

Time will not allow of my entering fully on the arguments
on either side at present. Those who wish to see all that
can be urged in favour of the tradition, will find it stated in
the Rev. George Williams's work entitled 'The Holy City,'
more especially in the Chapter on the Sepulchre, written by
the Rev. Professor Willis. Those whose tastes or reason
incline the other way will find the arguments against the
site tersely and logically summed up by Dr. Robinson, in
his 'Biblical Researches in Palestine.'

It may, however, be stated generally, that those who cling
to the traditions argue that Constantine, 300 years after the
event, must have had better means of arriving at a correct
conclusion than we can have, and would not have fixed on
that site without good reasons for the selection; and add that
since his time there has been no solution of continuity. On
the other hand, it is urged that the Bible narrative represents Christ as going from the judgment-seat—admitted to
be the Antonia — towards the country, — crucified outside
the walls, and laid in a rock-cut sepulchre nigh at hand;
whereas they contend that the present site was always
inside the walls—that to reach it he must have passed
through a great part of the city—that there is no rock in
the present sepulchre, &c.

The opponents of the present site also add that, if we can
now point to remains of ancient walls and buildings to the
northward of the present church, these indications must have
been ten times more distinct in the 4th century, before a
dozen of sieges and the rebuilding and alterations of fifteen

centuries had done so much to obliterate them. They contend that it is almost impossible that those who acted with Constantine could have been so ignorant of the Bible narrative as to place the sepulchre in what they must have seen was the middle of the old town, as it is of its modern successor.

These propositions are, of course, disputed by the opposite party, but it is easy to see that the real difficulty of the whole case is the want of a *tertium quid*. If this is not the sepulchre, the traditionalists ask, where is it? Nothing is more difficult than to prove a negative; and while there were no positive facts to rest upon, the argument was necessarily inconclusive, and probably incapable of settlement.

It was while the controversy was in this position that I became—I may say, almost by accident—entangled in its meshes; and in explaining to you how this came to pass, I trust you will pardon me if I speak more of myself than may be quite consistent with good taste. I would not do so did I not feel that by a personal narrative I can put the facts of the case more vividly before you, and in far less time, than I could by double the amount of impersonal circumlocution. If I succeed in this, I trust you will forgive the unwilling though apparent egotism.

During a long residence in India I occupied my leisure in studying the architecture of that glorious country, and applied myself to the investigation not only of the Buddhist and Hindoo, but to that of the Mahometan styles which had been practised there. I became perfectly familiar with the mosques of Agra and Delhi, and other great cities of the Moslem conquerors, and knew every form of tomb that had been used from the time of Kootub-ed-deen, the first conqueror, to that of the last Nawab of Lucknow. I had visited the mosques and tombs of Cairo and Egypt, and had acquainted myself with those of Persia, Syria, and Asia generally, in so far as was possible from the books then published. But in all my researches one building alone stood out strange and incomprehensible, and that was the so-called Mosque of Omar at Jerusalem. Mosque it certainly was not, for in its arrangements it transgressed the fundamental principles of mosque architecture. The essential definition of a mosque reduced to its simplest expression is that it is a wall at right angles to the direction of Mecca. The precept of the Koran is, "that all men, when they pray, shall turn towards the Kaaba," or holy house at Mecca, and consequently throughout the Moslem world indicators have been put up to enable the faithful to fulfil this condition. In India they face west, in Barbary east, in Syria south. It is true that when rich men or kings built mosques they frequently covered the face of this wall with arcades, to shelter the worshipper from the sun or rain. They enclosed it in a court, that his meditations might not be disturbed by the noises of the outside world. They provided it with fountains, that he might perform the required ablutions before prayer. But still the essential part of the mosque is the Mihrab or niche which points towards Mecca, and towards which when he bows, the worshipper knows that the Kaaba also is before him.

Now the building in question, so far from answering to this description, is an octagon, and with an entrance in each of the four faces fronting the Cardinal points of the compass, but, strange to say, with the principal entrance facing the south, or direction of Mecca, so that every

worshipper entering by it turns his back on the Holy
Kaaba — a sacrilege which any one who has lived long
among Moslems will easily feel and appreciate.

Had it been called the *Tomb* of Omar, I probably should
hardly have inquired further.
Tombs in the earlier ages of
the world were circular. They
afterwards became octagonal
and sometimes square, and
generally, after the Roman
period, were surmounted by
domes, as this building is.

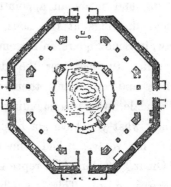

I had seen hundreds, I may
almost say thousands, of Moslem tombs in the East, differing in no very essential respect,

[No. 2.]

Plan of the Dome of Rock at Jerusalem.
From Catherwood and Arundale.
Scale 100 ft. to 1 in.

in so far as plan is concerned, from this one. Many
had four entrances, but generally, it must be confessed, the
door facing Mecca was closed, and ornamented with a
Mihrab or niche of prayer; but this was not essential, and
certainly not always the case.

Though therefore it might, in the then state of my
knowledge, have been classed among the tombs, there
unfortunately was no tradition or hint of any kind that
either Omar or any Mahometan saint or celebrity had been
buried beneath its dome.

If, therefore, it was neither mosque nor tomb, what was
it? My knowledge was at fault, and I could suggest no
answer.

While in this state of perplexity, I learned that Messrs.
Catherwood and Arundale, accompanied by Mr. Bonomi,

had gained access to the Haram area in 1833; had measured and drawn every part of the buildings within the
sacred enclosure; and that these gentlemen were then in
England. I, in consequence, obtained an introduction to
them, and made an appointment to meet them and see
their drawings at the house of Mr. Arundale's father-in-
law, in Soho Square, in December, 1846.

After turning over the drawings carefully more than
once, and examining them with care, I turned to Mr.
Arundale, who was standing by me, and said, "Do you
know what you have got here?"—"The Mosque of Omar,"
was his reply. "And who do you suppose built it?"—
"Omar." "Omar!" I repeated. "It is impossible he could
have done so. This is a Christian sepulchral building of
the time of Constantine. It can be no other than the
Church of the Holy Sepulchre."

I need hardly add that my new friends scarcely knew
whether I was serious or in joke in proposing so startling
an hypothesis. I urged them to publish the drawings.
They declined. "They had been to every publisher
in London — no one would look at them; they could
not afford to do it themselves." Finding them immove-
able on this head, I proposed to purchase the drawings,
and publish them. Finally we agreed to meet again on
the following Monday.

The week that intervened I spent in the library of the
British Museum, consulting every work on the subject to
which I could obtain a reference. Everything I learnt
confirmed me more and more in the conclusion I had
arrived at from the architecture; and consequently, when
we met, we soon came to terms. I agreed to pay a certain

price for such drawings as I wanted, which Mr. Arundale
was to furnish.   Immediately afterwards I set myself to
prepare for the publication of my work on the 'Ancient
Topography of Jerusalem,' which appeared in 1847.

Now, what I want to explain to you this evening is, what
were the data from which I arrived so suddenly at the
conclusion, that a building always supposed to be of Saracenic architecture, was really of Christian origin; and why,
after fifteen years, I still believe, more firmly than I did at
first, that the building popularly known as the Mosque
of Omar is, in reality, the sepulchral building which Constantine erected over what he believed to be the tomb of
Christ.

PART II.

ARCHITECTURE.

In attempting to explain the architectural peculiarities of
the buildings within the Haram area, I fear I must again
lay myself open to the charge of being too elementary.
But, in order that all may follow what I am about to
advance, this is probably indispensable.

Those who are familiar with the writings of architectural
critics of the last century will recollect how completely
the *litera scripta* prevailed over every other class of evidence in determining the age of buildings.   If a monkish
chronicler related that an abbey was burnt down, and
rebuilt from its foundations, during the wars of the Roses,
the antiquarians of that day saw nothing to invalidate this

statement in the circular arches of the nave, or the lancets of the choir. Either these peculiarities were caprices of the architect employed in the restoration, or proofs that all styles were or might have been practised simultaneously during the middle ages, in the same incongruous jumble as prevails at the present day.

The early writings of Britton first let in some light on this subject. In the multifarious buildings which he illustrated, it was generally perceived that a certain form of style agreed with a certain date. Mediæval chronicles, however, in almost every instance, exaggerated so absurdly both as to destructions and rebuildings—that, so long as they were appealed to, there were too many striking exceptions to this rule, to allow of the doctrine of styles being generally accepted in Britton's day.

Rickman* was the first who boldly dared to grapple with the subject. With very little knowledge of books, but a keen eye for style, he saw at a glance the value of the latter characteristic. Once he had grasped the idea, he set himself to work it out enthusiastically—invented a nomenclature, multiplied examples, and soon educed order out of chaos. Whewell and Willis followed in this path. The French, twenty years afterwards, caught up the idea, and soon surpassed us in the brilliancy of their classifications, and, at last, the Germans awoke to a sense of its importance.

As the case at present stands, it may be broadly asserted that, in every instance of conflicting evidence, an appeal to style is at once allowed to override the most minute and circumstantial written testimony. And now that the general

* The first edition of his work was published 1817.

chronometric scale has been determined upon and agreed to by antiquarians, few refer to the chronicles in which the history of the buildings is recorded, but are content, in the first instance at least, to fix dates from the styles alone.

If any lingering doubts exist in any mind on this subject, it is owing to the strange anomalous manner in which architecture is practised at the present day, and the confusion of styles we see at present around us. When we see Grecian, Saracenic, or Gothic buildings rising at the same time,— Norman, Early English, and Perpendicular styles practised by the same architect at the same hour,—it requires some knowledge and no little effort to feel quite sure that something of the same kind may not have existed at some previous period. But there is no fact in the history of art more certain than that this absurd practice arose in Europe in the 16th century; that it did not exist in any country at any age previous to that time; and consequently no argument derived from it can be applied to earlier buildings, or in other lands where common sense still governs the design of buildings, as it does other forms of the fine or useful arts.

In so far as Gothic architecture is concerned, this doctrine is now universally admitted as regards every country of Europe; but many are not aware that the same is true of the classic styles,—of the Saracenic,—the Indian, and of every true style. In fact, progress easily perceived, and as easily registered, was the law of development of every style of architecture in Europe, down to the great revival in the 16th century, and is the law to this time in some of the remote countries of the East, where the influence of the round-hatted race is not yet supreme.

All this would have been perceived and acknowledged long ago, but that it has happened that, since the discovery of the chronometric scale by style, Gothic art has occupied the attention of the public almost to the exclusion of every other. The Pagan styles in particular are an abomination in the eyes of nine-tenths of those who turn their attention to architectural art in this country.

Personally I have been fortunate in the accident that my travels have led me to take a wider view of the subject, and repeatedly I have had occasion to investigate the gradual progress of the Roman, Byzantine, and Saracenic styles, and need hardly add that their development follows the same identical law as has been so successfully applied to the mediæval styles, and that it is quite as easy to determine dates from an appeal to the *Ipsissima Saxa* in them, as it is in regard to Gothic buildings.

Time will not admit of my attempting to prove this proposition on the present occasion, nor is it required, as, till controverted, it may be assumed as self-evident. Nor will it be necessary to go very far back in order to bring our knowledge to bear on those buildings at Jerusalem which are the subject of the present investigation. It will not, for instance, be needed to point out the steps by which the Roman style was gradually elaborated out of a not very lawful marriage of the Grecian and Etruscan styles. So long as Grecian mythology and Grecian art were the fashion, the Romans copied Grecian pillars and their trabeate architecture in their Temples. In their aqueducts and amphitheatres the Romans were, however, so familiar with the arch, and found it so constructively convenient, that their natural tendency was always in that direction; and the moment the pressure of religious feeling was removed, they swung towards it with a rapidity which is startling.

From the time of the building of the Flavian Amphi-theatre, till that of the Maxentian Basilica, we can trace this tendency step by step; but it is not necessary to do that now, as we have, in the palace of Diocletian at Spalatro, a typical example, which is sufficient for our present purposes. That building was completed, as we now find it, by that emperor, before his death in 304.

In the so-called Temple of Esculapius, in that palace, we find the Greek style and Grecian templar arrangements perfect in all their parts, though debased in detail.

In the octagon building which Diocletian erected, probably as his own sepulchre, we find a far greater deviation from the classical type.   In the peristyle between these two buildings we have in the central arch (woodcut No. 3), leading to the principal apartments of the palace, the whole entablature, cornice, frieze, and architrave, bent into an arch, though, on each side of it, the entablature still retains its original form. On each side of the court the architrave alone forms an arch from pillar to pillar, resting direct on the capital.   The entablature runs horizontally above, as forming a cornice to the wall which these arches support.

In the gateways and other utilitarian parts of the building, all the ordinances of classical art are set at defiance (wood-cut No. 4).   The pillars have become mere ornamental shafts supported on brackets, their capitals portions of a string-course, and the whole thus becomes a decorative screen, such as—*mutatis mutandis*—is frequently found in the middle ages.   We have thus in this palace an essentially transitional specimen of architectural art.   The old style exists nowhere

Peristyle in Palace of Spalatro.   From Sir Gardner Wilkinson's 'Dalmatia.'

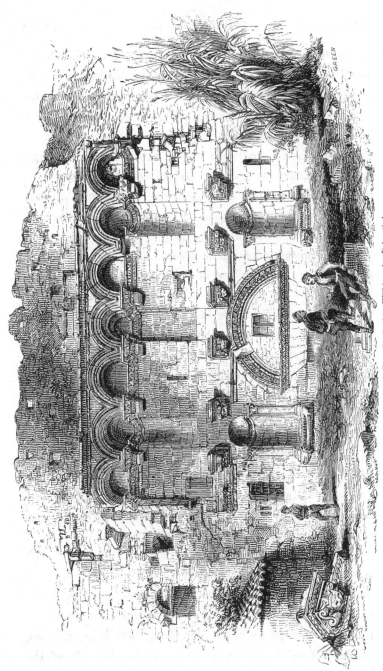

Golden Gateway at Spalatro.   From Sir Gardner Wilkinson's 'Dalmatia.'

[No. 4.]

in anything like purity except in the Temple. In all the secular or sepulchral parts the tendency is towards something new; and though the details are sometimes old, the forms are much more similar to those we find elaborated some centuries afterwards.

It is much to be regretted that we have no similar example about a century later, and we are obliged to go on to the time of Justinian (A.D. 527-564) before we get such a group of buildings as shall enable us to be quite sure that we understand the style in all its details. His buildings, however, at Constantinople, those erected in his day at Ravenna and elsewhere in Italy, and at Salonica, enable us to speak positively of what the style had become during his reign.

In the beginning of the 6th century the proportions and the spacing of the pillars had become anything that the constructive exigencies of the case demanded. The hollow line of the classic capital was replaced by a bulging one, and the Corinthian acanthus had given place to a conventional form of vegetation which it is difficult to identify (woodcuts 5 and 6). But the most striking peculiarity of the completed transition is, that the horizontal entablature had disappeared, and given place to an essentially arched style. In short, the ancient trabeate Pagan art was gone, and had been replaced by a modern arched Byzantine style, differing from the older one in all essential features.

Between those two epochs we have several buildings, such as the Church of St. John Studios, at Constantinople, A.D. 463, and the Eski d'Jami, at Salonica, built certainly within the limits of the 5th century, which are sufficient to mark the steps by which the change was being effected, though not in themselves sufficient to fix the date of the transition. But other examples are daily coming to light which may enable us to be more precise at some future period.

[No. 5.]   Lower Order of the Church of Sta. Sophia (A.D. 536–540).   From Salzenburg.

It is scarcely necessary to add that we know exactly what was the style of architecture of the Roman Empire before the time of Diocletian. After the time of Justinian also we are no longer in doubt, the examples being sufficient to prove that no retrocession took place at any subsequent epoch.

Now, what I want to point out to you this evening is that

the buildings known at Jerusalem as the Dome of the Rock
and the Golden Gateway were erected between the epochs of

Diocletian and Justinian,—near-
er the former than the latter.
And if I make this clear I feel
sure you will agree with me in
ascribing them to Constantine.
But before proceeding to this,
let me pause one moment to
explain to you exactly what the
buildings are of which I propose
to speak.

[No. 6.]   Upper Order of Sta. Sophia (A.D.
536-540). From Salzenburg.

The principal of these is the
octagonal building popularly
known as the Mosque of Omar, but more correctly designated
the "Dome of the Rock." It stands on a platform of its own
in the midst of the sacred enclosure known as the Haram
Area, and is the most conspicuous object in all views of
Jerusalem, especially those taken from the eastward, or
that side on which the Mount of Olives is situated.

The second is the Golden Gateway, a festal portal inserted
in the eastern wall not far from the first-named building.

The third is the Mosque el Aksah, situated near the
middle of that part of the Haram area which was formerly
occupied by Herod's Temple.

The Church of the Holy Sepulchre in the city ought to
form a fourth in the series, but that it has no *locus standi* in
an architectural argument. Its most strenuous supporters
cannot point out a single detail or constructive peculiarity
that belongs to an age anterior to that of the Crusades; and
therefore, whatever may be said in defence of its claims to be

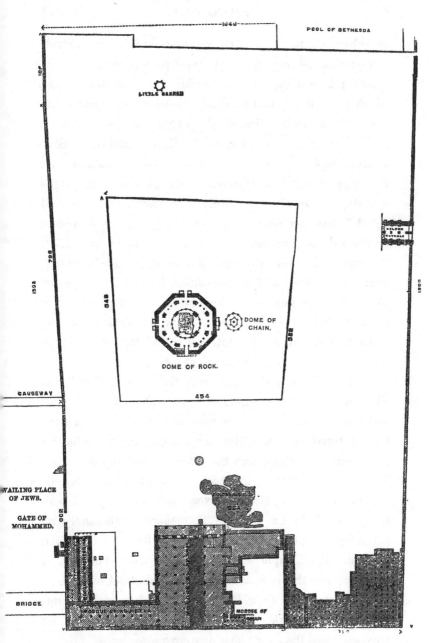

POOL OF BETHESDA

LITTLE SAKHRA

DOME OF CHAIN.

DOME OF ROCK.

454

CAUSEWAY

WAILING PLACE OF JEWS.

GATE OF MOHAMMED.

SEA

BRIDGE

[No. 7.]   Plan of Haram Area at Jerusalem, showing the buildings which now exist.

considered the successor of Constantine's building, no support can be obtained from its architectural peculiarities.

The principal one of these buildings is the first named, which is practically that on which the whole argument turns. The Mahometan tradition since the Crusades assumes that it covers the site of the Altar, or the Holy of Holies, of Solomon's Temple, or the rock on which modern tradition says the angel stood who appeared to David when the plague was stayed. But it need hardly be remarked that the word "rock" does not occur either in the Bible, or Josephus, or the Talmud, nor indeed anywhere else in ancient times, as connected either with the altar or Holy of Holies. It seems to be wholly a Moslem tradition, but has been repeated so often in the present controversy that most persons have come to believe that there is some foundation for the belief that this rock represents the site of the altar, though there does not seem to be any whatever.

What we know of the altar from the Bible is that it was situated on the threshing-floor of Araunah, and this rugged and uneven rock certainly never was and never could have been a threshing-floor under any circumstances. What we know from Josephus is that the altar was built up of natural unhewn stones which no iron tool had touched (B. J. v. 5, § 6), and the Talmud repeats this even more distinctly and positively (Middoth, iii. 4). So that there is absolutely no authority, except the modern tradition, for connecting the altar and the Temple with any rock. Even, however, if this were not the case, and the altar did stand on a rock, we shall presently show that this particular specimen was altogether outside the Temple area, and therefore could not have sustained the altar under any circumstances.

The building which encloses the rock is an octagon 155
feet in diameter, in the centre of which is a circular apart-
ment surmounted by a dome measuring 65 feet across in-
ternally, and under which nearly the whole floor is occupied
by a great mass of living rock rising about 8 feet above
the level of the aisles, and in that rock is a cave, regarding
the use or origin of which the Moslems are by no means
clear. The central dome is supported by four great piers,
between each of which are three pillars supporting arches
springing direct from their capitals. Beyond this the
external space of 35 feet is divided into two aisles by a
screen of eight piers and sixteen pillars, and nearly 400
feet in length, which is the most interesting and most un-
altered part of the building, and that consequently on which
the architectural argument mainly hinges. The external
walls have been a good deal altered by necessary and
decorative repairs at various periods.

The first thing to be remarked in the screen is that the pillars
are mounted on stools or sub-bases, as in the octagon building at Spalatro, and as we find them in the buildings of the
next century at Salonica (woodcut No. 8) and Constantinople,
but as they ceased to be in Justinian's time and afterwards.

The capitals are of a simple Corinthian order of Diocletian's day, which had disappeared long before Justinian's
reign. Above them still ranges the old classical entablature, but with this remarkable alteration. Although of
wood, it would have looked crushingly heavy if maintain-
ing its classical depth across pillars spaced eight diameters
apart. The architrave is consequently omitted, and represented only by a square block over each pillar supporting
the frieze and cornice, of fairly classical design, and over

[No 8.]   Arches in St. Demetrius at Salonica, about A.D. 500.

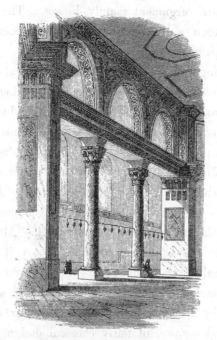

[No. 9.]   View in Aisle of Dome of Rock.   From a drawing by Catherwood.

this comes a bold discharging arch, which again supports
a cornice which was originally apparently classical, but is
now hid in more modern details.

We have thus in this building, in the centre, circular
arches resting directly on the capitals, as at Spalatro. We
have in the screen arches resting on an entablature supported
by architrave blocks, but we have not the third stage, which
became universal in the 5th century, and continued generally
throughout Justinian's reign, of arches springing direct from
architrave blocks without any intervening entablature.

[No. 10.]   Order of the Dome of the Rock. From a drawing by Arundale.

Look at it indeed which way you will, it is impossible to
conceive a more essentially transitional example than this—

the horizontal trabeate architecture of Pagan Rome strug-
gling to retain its position against the Christian arcuate style
by which it was so soon to be superseded. After this period,
so far as I know, there is no single instance of a horizontal
cornice being used as a decorative feature anywhere. It died
with Constantine, and we here witness its last expiring agony.

Any one who is familiar with the gradual development of
styles, and is in the habit of noting the phenomena that mark
transitional epochs, would probably be satisfied with this
evidence ; but it may not unnaturally be asked, " Are there
any other buildings of the same age with which this can be
compared ? "

Anteriorly, perhaps, the best for the purpose is the octagonal temple or tomb building above alluded to, which
Diocletian erected in his palace at Spalatro. It is in all
essential respects identical with this building at Jerusalem,
except that the first-named emperor, like a good Pagan, put
his colonnade outside his building in the form of a peristyle ;
while Constantine, like a good Christian, put his inside, in
the shape of an aisle.

Then we have the Lateran Baptistery which Constantine
built for his own sepulchre, and which, though very much
smaller, is in its architectural arrangement essentially
identical with this one. So is the tomb which he built for
Sta. Constantia his daughter. The church which he built
at Antioch was octagonal, and, so far as we can make out
from the imperfect description of Eusebius,* it also was
very like this Dome of the Rock.

In the 4th century and the next we have several churches

---

* Vita Constantini, l. iii.

bearing a strong family resemblance to this one, such as San Stefano Rotondo at Rome, the Baptistery at Nocera, and the San Giorgio at Salonica, which, though astylar, is interesting as showing how prevalent the circular domical type of church was in the 4th century of our era.

When we come down to the age of Justinian, we find quite a different state of affairs. We have octagonal churches it is true, such as San Vitale at Ravenna, and the church of Sergius and Bacchus, now known as the little St. Sophia, at Constantinople. But in these the choir and apse have become essential and integral parts of the design. The Corinthian capital is gone. The arch rests on the capital or the architrave block, and the whole style is complete in itself, and as essentially different from the old classical style as the Gothic of Edward III. is from the Norman of the Conqueror.

It need hardly be added that in those days retrocession in style was absolutely unknown, and those who contend that this building was erected by the Moslems, or by any other parties after the time of Justinian, have got to point out the existence of any one building in any part of the world, or in any subsequent age, which resembles this one either in design or style. Such a building may exist, but of this I feel certain—that it has not yet been seen by modern eye, or at least described by modern pen, and till it is brought forward we may treat *de non apparentibus* as *non existentibus.**

---

* I have never answered the argument of Mr. Lewin against my views as expressed in his several publications, though it would be easy to do so, for this reason,—that he admits that the Dome of the Rock may have been built in the 4th century (Sketch of Jerusalem, p. 150, and repeated in the Topography of Jerusalem). He probably fancies he sees some way out of the

Nor will it do to suggest, as some have attempted to do, that these classical forms were borrowed by the Moslems from some earlier buildings. In the first place, we know from Arculfus, at the end of the 7th century (after this building is said to have been completed), that all the Christian buildings were standing and entire. But more than this, the extent of it quite precludes any such supposition. If it were a portico of four or six pillars, with twenty or thirty feet of entablature, anything might be assumed. But, confining the argument to the aisle screen alone, eight piers, sixteen pillars, and 400 feet of entablature mitreing at all sorts of angles, and fitting everywhere without any appearance of contrivance or adjustment, is a phenomenon not to be explained away. This, however, is only a small part of the whole evidence.

The whole arrangement and design of the building is utterly unlike anything we know of Saracenic architecture, and there is a beauty of proportion and an appropriateness of detail which we do not find in their works, till their style was thoroughly elaborated into a whole, after the crusades.

On the other hand, it is just such a building as we should expect to find emanating from Constantine's order that "the church may surpass all others in beauty, and that the details of the building may be such that the finest structure of any city of the Empire may be excelled by this." *

So far as we can judge, this precept has been literally obeyed, and, taken in conjunction with the details of style just pointed out, ought to suffice to settle the controversy.

---

dilemma in which he thus places himself, though he does not explain it. So far as I am concerned, it is granting all I ask. He writes as if he were my opponent, I accept him as the best of my allies.

* Eusebius, Vita Constantin. iii. 32.

If, in short, Constantine did not build this Dome of the Rock, our architectural science is a delusion, unless some one can bring forward new data from which new conclusions must be drawn. But the architectural world has been tolerably well explored, and there is little chance of this; and something very distinct and clear would be required to upset what we already really do know, and all which points to the conclusion above indicated.

The first proposition—that this building was not erected before the time of Diocletian—probably all will admit.

The second—that it was built before the time of Justinian—appears to me as undeniable and as capable of proof.

The third—that it was built very nearly at the beginning of the epoch intervening between the reigns of the two monarchs indicated—I feel convinced will be admitted by all who are familiar with its architectural peculiarities and will take the trouble to compare them with the buildings at Spalatro and those of Constantine pointed out above.

If this be so, the argument might be allowed to stop here. For whatever historical difficulties might at first sight appear to militate against these conclusions, we may rest assured will melt away when fairly grappled with. If I have correctly appreciated the architectural argument, it is final, and must be swept away before it can be denied that the Dome of the Rock is a building of the age of Constantine the Great.

GOLDEN GATEWAY.

IF we turn to the Golden Gateway, we find architectural
phenomena precisely similar in all essential respects to those
just pointed out as characterizing the Dome of the Rock, but
varied as might be expected from the diverse purposes of the

[No. 11.]   Interior of the Golden Gateway.   From a drawing by Catherwood.
Originally published in Fisher's 'Oriental Album.'

two buildings. In the interior of the Gateway the central
arches spring direct from the architrave blocks, and support flat domes with pendentives. These are an Eastern
form of art, regarding which it is difficult to find parallel
examples in our books of architecture, which are almost
exclusively devoted to Western examples. The argument

[No. 12.]   Order of the Golden Gateway.   From a drawing by Arundale.

as to the date of the building rests therefore principally,
in so far as the interior is concerned, on the quasi-classical
cornice which runs along the wall on both sides. It is
here used merely as an ornamental feature, like the cornice
(woodcut No. 9) under the discharging arches in the Dome

of the Rock, and is evidently of the same age and style, and, like it, used not as a constructive necessity, but as a reminiscence of the old but expiring style of classical art. A horizontal cornice may occasionally be found used for constructive purposes as late as the time of Justinian, though of course with less classical detail than is found here; but no instance is known in which it was employed for merely ornamental purposes after the 4th century, to which these two buildings must consequently be ascribed from this cause alone, till some example to the contrary can be pointed out.

This would be apparent at a glance to every one, if it were not that the Dome has been used as a place of worship for fifteen centuries, first by Christians, then by Moslems. During the crusades the Christians recovered it, and made it the Patriarchal Church of Jerusalem, and again the Mahometans adapted it to their own rites. It has been so altered by all these changes in many of its details, that the original form and construction are not at once apparent. The Golden Gateway, on the other hand, having never been used as a place of worship by the followers of either religion, remains now as originally erected.

If any one will take the trouble to look back and compare this capital and entablature, or those shown in the woodcuts No. 10 and No. 12, with those from the Church of St. Sophia (woodcuts No. 5 and No. 6), it must be evident how much more nearly the two examples at Jerusalem approach the classical type than the two from Constantinople. The two first named would hardly be remarked as anachronisms in Diocletian's palace at Spalatro, or in buildings of the 4th century at Rome. The two last quoted exhibit a completed

style from which all true classical feeling had been entirely
banished. To assert that the Mahometans after Justinian's
time went back to the practice of the more classical type
of art, is one of the most startling assertions that can well
be hazarded, and is not warranted by any experience in any
age in the architectural history of the world anterior to the
16th century.

If, on the contrary, we compare the Jerusalem capitals
with those of the Church
of St. John Studios at
Constantinople (wood-
cut 13), built in the
year 463, it will be seen
at a glance how much
more nearly those two
approach in style to one
another than they do to
those from Sta. Sophia.
We must also bear in
mind how much more
slowly the style changes
in sacred than it does in
secular buildings, and
make some allowance
for the provincial situ-
ation of Jerusalem as
compared with the me-
tropolis, where the clas-
sical tradition would re-
main longer in force. If
we make a fair allowance

[No. 13.]   Pillar in Church of St. John, Constantinople.

for these circumstances, it seems hardly possible to arrive
at any other conclusion than that the Golden Gateway is
an older example than the capital of St. John, or than the
buildings of about the same epoch at Salonica, and *à fortiori*
very much more ancient than Sta. Sophia at Constantinople.

Externally, especially in the inner face of the Golden
Gateway, we have an entire entablature, architrave, frieze,
and cornice, bent as at Spalatro (ante, woodcut No. 3), and
arching from pillar to pillar; a peculiarity which I believe
I am correct in stating is never found in any building after
the 4th century, but is eminently characteristic of the age of
Constantine.

If we look only at the style, it is true it may be said
the Gateway is somewhat more modern than the Dome
of the Rock. But in the same sense it may be asserted that
the Flavian Amphitheatre is more advanced in style than
are temples which we know were erected in the age of the
Antonines or Aurelian, nearly a century after its date. In
secular buildings men were bound by no trammels. In religious edifices certain forms were sacred, and it was with
difficulty they could be dispensed with.

It is hardly worth while, however, re-arguing the question
at any length, as all the same arguments apply to it as have
just been urged with reference to the Dome of the Rock; and
in so far as their architecture is concerned, they must stand
or fall together. It is, indeed, less necessary to re-argue the
question with regard to the Golden Gateway, as no one has
yet ventured to contend that it was built by the Mahometans
or by any one so late as the time of Justinian. The tendency
of the arguments as concerns this building has been quite in
the opposite direction. Some ascribe it to Herod, some even

to Solomon, but the best judges range between Herod and some nameless builder in the 5th or 6th century.*

View of Golden Gateway from the Haram Area.   From a drawing by Arundale.

[No. 14.]

---

* "Ces derniers fragments (the exterior of the Golden Gateway, and the frontispiece of the Gate Huldah) ne peuvent être que du temps d'Hérode le Grand, ou que du temps d'Adrien, ou que du temps de Constantin."—Viollet le Duc.   Entretiens d'Arch., p. 225.

Strangely enough, however, some of those who contend most stoutly against the larger building having been erected by Constantine, are willing to admit that the gateway may be of the 4th or 5th century; though those who admit this seem hardly to be aware of the consequences of such an admission, inasmuch as they have failed to suggest who put it there, and for what purpose. It was not, and, from its arrangements, could not be, a gate of the city; it was not, and could not be, a gate of the "accursed Temple" of the Jews, which did not extend nearly to this spot, and which certainly was not rebuilt in the 4th or 5th century.*

If, therefore, it was not either of these, what could it be but the festal entrance described by Eusebius as leading to the Basilica of Constantine?

Till some clear and credible answer is given to this inquiry, this gateway remains a piece of evidence in favour of the views I am advocating, which cannot be negatived, and which in itself goes very far to settle the question at issue.

---

* De Vogüé, in his great work entitled 'Le Temple de Jérusalem,' p. 64 et seq., argues that this gateway is a Christian Byzantine building of the 5th or 6th century. I think he hardly sufficiently appreciates the rapid progression of style belonging to local position and quasi-secular purpose, and makes it consequently a century too modern. As far as my argument is concerned, this is not of the least consequence. In making this admission, he grants all I could ask him to concede. The Christians in this age did not build, or attempt to rebuild, the "accursed Temple" of the Jews; and this gateway, if built by them, certainly led to one of their churches, and, if so, there is an end to all further argument till some new reason for the existence of the gateway is suggested.

It may also be added that De Vogüé insists strongly on the existence of the Christian monogram on the architrave blocks above the capitals, though it is partially obliterated. My own observations entirely agree with this, though the cross is so nearly cut away that it would hardly do to found any argument upon it; and fortunately it is not needed, the architecture being in itself quite sufficient to fix the age of the Gateway.

No remains now exist of the basilica to which the Golden Gateway led. Some of the pillars which once adorned it are no doubt to be found among those forming screens, and decorating buildings, in the Haram area or elsewhere; and some portions of its cornice are used as stringcourses in the facade of the present Church of the Holy Sepulchre, but nothing remains *in situ*.

One circumstance, however, may be mentioned as bearing on the site of the Golden Gateway. In describing the basilica, Eusebius* speaks of the side aisles, " as well those under ground as those above ground "—meaning evidently thereby that the upper galleries were approached on the level from the outside like those of the nearly contemporary churches of S. Lorenzo and Sta. Agnese at Rome.

This fact is interesting here, as it accounts for the position of the Golden Gateway some fifteen feet below the general level of the Haram area—a circumstance which it would not be easy to account for without reference to this fact, but which is just one of those numerous confirmations that are sure to spring up when the investigation is on the right track. But the great fact, which no one seems able or inclined to dispute, is that the Golden Gateway is a Christian building erected before the time of Justinian. If so, what is it? If any one can supply a satisfactory answer to this question, it will materially aid a fast declining cause; until it is supplied, the argument halts.

---

* Vita Constantini, l. iii. 27.

[No. 15.]   View in the Mosque el Aksah at Jerusalem.   From a drawing by Arundale.

EL AKSAH.

WHEN from these buildings we turn to the Mosque el
Aksah, which is the third on our list, we find ourselves
in a new world altogether. With the exception of two
or three capitals borrowed from the church of Justinian
after its destruction, and fitting most awkwardly to their
places, there is not a classical feature about the place:
no entablature running from pillar to pillar, or along the

walls; no round constructive arches anywhere; nothing in plan or detail to recall the features of Pagan Rome. On the contrary, the piers are as widely spaced as in the late Gothic buildings; the arches all pointed; and the whole arrangement of that light, airy nature which is so characteristic of the Saracenic style in Europe and Western Asia. Whoever built it, of this fact at least we may feel certain: that two or three centuries at least elapsed between the erection of the Dome of the Rock and the Aksah, and that the latter is the more modern. It would be as reasonable to assert that the naves of Rochester and Canterbury —as we now find them—were erected by the same architect, in the same age, as to ascribe these two buildings to one time.

At the same time, the evidence both architectural and historical is amply sufficient to prove that the Aksah was built by Abd el Malek ibn Merwan, and finished in the year 72 Hejira, A.D. 791. The evidence is so clear and distinct on this point that it would never have been called in question but for a strange error which has crept into the controversy. Richardson, in his Travels (A.D. 1814), suggested it might be Justinian's church as described by Procopius, and the error has been propagated industriously, and will probably continue to be so. The following reasons, among many, may suffice to dispel the illusion.

The Aksah certainly stands on the site of the Jewish Temple. Now, we know that spot to have been held accursed by the Christians, from the time of Julian's attempt to rebuild it, till the time at least of Eutychius in the 9th century,* " because "—as he expresses it—" our Lord had

---

* Eutychii Ann., vol. ii. p. 284.

said in the Holy Gospel, 'Behold your house shall be left unto you desolate;' and again, 'There shall not be left one stone upon another that shall not be cast down and laid waste.'" We consequently feel certain that Justinian did not build his Mary Church within its accursed precincts.

The great difficulty which Justinian experienced in building his church, and the wonder of it when accomplished, was—according to Procopius—the vaulted substructure which he was obliged to erect in order to get a level place on which to build his superstructure. Now the substructures of the Aksah, in so far as they are of masonry, are of Herod's time, and not erected by Justinian at all. But the greater part of the building rests on the rock, which crops up to the surface in some places within it, and in others is only a few feet below the floor.

There is no apse to the plan, and neither the details nor the ordinance of the Aksah are those of Justinian's other buildings—nor, indeed, those of a Christian church, though not unlike those of the mosque at Cordova, and other Moslem buildings of about that age. It never would have been assumed to have been built for Christian purposes, had its arrangements been studied with care, and with the view of assigning them their true place in the series.

In addition to this negative evidence, we have the positive and repeated assurance of the Mahometan historians, who ought to be the best authorities on such a subject, that the Aksah was built by Abd el Malek.

They give its dimensions, and describe its details with a minuteness which leaves no doubt as to their meaning. Thus Jelal ed deen says, "There are in the mosque fifteen chapels to match the chapel of the Sakrah." There are just

seven spaces on each side of the Aksah, and the chapel
opposite the Mosque of Omar would complete the number.

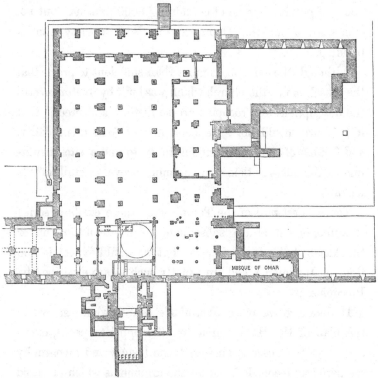

[No. 16.]   Plan of the Mosque el Aksah at Jerusalem.   Scale 100 ft. to 1 in.

And, again, the same author says, "The Mosque el Aksah is
divided into seven compartments (aisles), supported by piers
and columns, among which forty-five are columns, and
thirty-three are pillars,"* which is the exact number given
in Catherwood's plan, and numerous other details are given
which leave no mistake as to the building they are
describing.

Besides this, we have the direct testimony of the French

---

* Jelal ed deen, translated by Reynolds, p. 191.

Bishop Arculfus (A.D. 700), who describes the Saracens as having then erected, *on the ruins of the Temple*, a square house of prayer, capable of containing 3000 persons,* but not one word about the Dome of the Rock or any similar building.

Although the evidence is more than sufficient to prove that the Aksah is not the church which was built by Justinian, still the descriptions of Procopius are so distinct and precise that it evidently could not have been distant from this locality, and fortunately we have not far to go to find a site answering in the most satisfactory manner to every detail of his narrative.

To the eastward of the Temple area there exists a series of vaults, of a style long subsequent to the date of those under the Aksah, but very similar to what we would expect in the time of Justinian,† and are exactly such as are described by Procopius.

If therefore we place Justinian's church where shown in the plan of the Haram area (on the opposite page), every exigency of the case is answered, the history and topography are perfectly reconciled, and all the arguments which are used to prove that the Aksah was Justinian's church are as applicable to the one close at hand.

This determination however raises another and most important series of questions.

Why did Justinian build his church in this quarter of the town at all. Why erect it "secus porticum Salomonis," as Antoninus expresses it? ‡

---

* Acta Sanctorum Ord. Bened., sæc. iii. pt. ii. p. 346.

† Williams's Holy City, vol ii., p. 375. "A section of these vaults is given by Mr. Fergusson, p. 121, who also ascribes them to Justinian, and is by accident right."

‡ Iter. ch. xxiii.

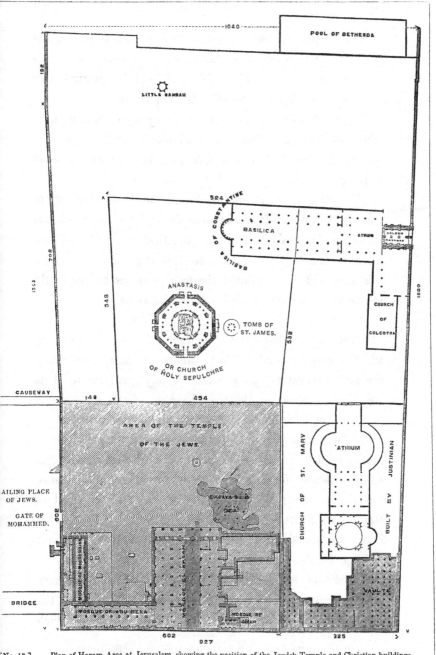

POOL OF BETHESDA

LITTLE SAKRAH

BASILICA OF CONSTANTINE

BASILICA

ATRIUM

GOLDEN GATEWAY

ANASTASIS

TOMB OF ST. JAMES.

CHURCH OF COLCOTRA

OR CHURCH OF HOLY SEPULCHRE

CAUSEWAY

AREA OF THE TEMPLE OF THE JEWS.

CHURCH OF ST. MARY

ATRIUM

BUILT BY JUSTINIAN

WAILING PLACE OF JEWS.

GATE OF MOHAMMED.

EXCAVATED DEA

MOSQUE OF MEHKEBE

MOSQUE EL AKSAY

MOSQUE OF OMAR

VAULTS

BRIDGE

MOSQUE OF ABU BEKA

[No. 17.] Plan of Haram Area at Jerusalem, showing the position of the Jewish Temple and Christian buildings.

If the Sepulchre and the scenes of the Passion were in the town where they are now shown, why did he not erect his church where the Sta. Maria Maggiore and Sta. Maria Latina now stand, in close proximity to the Sepulchre ?

Why seek so difficult a site, requiring such substructions, when abundance of level ground was available near the sacred Christian localities, and far from the accursed Temple of the Jews ?

The only answer, it appears to me, that can be given to these questions is—It was because the Dome of the Rock was then the Anastasis, and because the Basilica of Constantine and the Church of Golgotha were close at hand, that he chose this site, and so completed the four churches so frequently afterwards enumerated by mediæval historians.

There is another little building in the Haram area, which it may be worth while to allude to before concluding the architectural argument ; not for any great merit of its own, but as showing the worthlessness of the Mahometan traditions regarding the origin of the Dome of the Rock.

To the eastward of that building there is a small duodec-agonal edifice, known as the Dome of the Chain. As it has a kibleh facing Mecca, it probably was built by the Moslems, and their present tradition is that it was built by Abd el Malek, as a model, before erecting the Dome of the Rock.* Every feature shows it to be more modern; but the most striking incident is, that all its pillars and capitals are borrowed from some edifice of Justinian's, which must have been destroyed before it was commenced. Whereas, in the Dome of the Rock, there is not one capital or detail which

---

* During the Crusades it was called the Church of St. James.

can be said to have been borrowed from any building of
that age. The Aksah, and the Dome of the Chain, tell a
very different tale, being almost wholly made up of fragments
of Christian edifices, which had been destroyed before they
were completed, at least in their present form.

We know, from the testimony of Arculfus, that all the
four great Christian churches were standing in his day, and
no complaint made of any destruction or appropriation by
the Mahometans up to the year 700 at all events. We
learn the same thing from the narrative of the monk
Bernhard, A.D. 870. From their testimony, therefore, we
may appreciate the value of the Mahometan tradition as
to this little edifice. As it is built out of the remains of
a building of Justinian's, most probably his Mary Church,
which stood close by, it could hardly be erected before the
end of the 9th century. Yet they universally ascribe it to
Abd el Malek in the 7th, and place its date before that
of a building which has not a trace of any architecture of
Justinian's age in its composition.

It would be easy to carry this architectural argument to
a much greater extent than I have ventured to do ; but,
without more illustrations than could easily be exhibited,
or without presuming more knowledge, on your part, of the
architecture of that age, than I have any right to assume,
I fear I should hardly make myself intelligible. You
must therefore bear with me when I assert, even if it
should be a little too dogmatically, the conclusion I have
arrived at on this subject.

Of late years I have had several times occasion to go over
this subject when writing the architectural history of that

age, without any reference to the buildings at Jerusalem, and every time has strengthened my conviction that the Dome of the Rock, and the Golden Gateway, are buildings which, taking the widest margin, cannot possibly be dated before Diocletian's time, nor after Justinian's, and are, in fact, transitional specimens of the age of Constantine, exhibiting that struggle between the Pagan and Christian styles which characterised also the religious history of that age;—that the Aksah is a building of the first century of the Hejira, and the Dome of the Chain even more modern.

If this is so, it seems impossible to escape the conclusion that the Dome of the Rock is the identical building which Constantine erected over the Tomb of Christ, and the Golden Gateway the festal entrance to the Basilica, which he also erected alongside of it.

The difficulty cannot be got over by assuming that, though built in the 4th century, the Dome of the Rock may have been built by some other Christian monarch, and for some other purpose.

In the first place, it is one of the most important and magnificent buildings in the East, if not the most splendid ; and it could not have been smuggled into existence without being noticed by one of the numerous writers who speak of Jerusalem in that age.

In the next place, it is the most singular building in the whole world ; no other edifice, either Christian or Saracenic, is built over a living rock, which occupies the whole of its floor, which is, in fact, the cause and object of its building ; and even if it could be shown that a hundred or a thousand ordinary churches were erected in Palestine at that age, this consequently would still have been the most remarkable.

Lastly—neither Arculfus nor any historian mentions this building, unless they describe it as the Church of the Sepulchre.

We thus come back to the same point; and if it can be shown that it was built in or about the 4th century, the conclusion seems inevitable that it must be the original church of Constantine.

PART III.

HISTORY.

In order fully to appreciate the cogency of the architectural argument just enunciated, two things are needful: first, that you should be fully impressed with the truth of the proposition that style is sufficient in itself to settle such a question as this ; and, secondly, you ought to be sufficiently familiar with the details of the buildings under discussion, and with the progress of the particular style in which they are erected, to be able to follow the argument regarding them.

The first, I might perhaps presume upon in such an audience as this—and perhaps, also, on the second—were the buildings in question Gothic in detail; and I might, in consequence, stop here. But, even then, the argument might appear to many of you to lead only to an inexplicable dilemma, unless it could be shown that the historical record agreed, generally at least, with the architectural facts. Happily, there is no difficulty about this, except that the time allotted to me will force me to be brief, and to allude only to the more salient points in the story, referring those who desire more details to the various works I have published on the subject.

The history of the Holy Sepulchre naturally begins with Eusebius, who, as the friend and associate of Constantine, speaks with the authority of an eye-witness; and though his language is more rhetorical than is desirable, still there is nothing in what he says which may not be easily understood when the true localities are once ascertained.*

He first relates how impious men had covered up the cave with earth, and erected a temple to Venus on the mound so raised. When this was removed, he exclaims, "It was astonishing to see the rock standing out erect and alone on a level place, and having only one cavern in it, lest, had there been many, the miracle of him who overcame death should have been obscured." The cave being found, the Emperor commands "That a house of prayer should be erected round the Saviour's tomb, on a scale of rich and lavish magnificence which may surpass all others in beauty and that the details of the building be such that the finest structure in any city of the empire may be excelled by this.' Then, lest there should be any mistake about the locality, he adds, "Accordingly, on the very spot which witnessed the Saviour's sufferings, a new Jerusalem was constructed, *over against* the one so celebrated of old. It was *opposite* the city that the Emperor began to rear a monument of the Saviour's victory over death, with rich and lavish magnificence." (Woodcut, ante, p. 2.)

Having completed his description of the church erected

---

* The narrative which follows, and the quotations in the text, are taken from the 'Vita Constantini,' l. iii., ch. 25 and 35, and the parallel passages in the 'Theophania' of the same author.

over the Sepulchre, he then proceeds to describe the Basilica which adjoins it. This was of the usual form, five-aisled, and with a circular apse, with an entrance towards the east, in front of which was a portal opening on a broad agora or place where fairs might be held, or where refreshments or relics could be sold to pilgrims.

If we turn to the buildings I have just been describing,* it would be difficult to find words representing them with more correctness than those I have just quoted; whereas, if we apply those words, or indeed any expression of Eusebius, to the present buildings, there is nothing which can be made in any way applicable. Its defenders are obliged to have recourse to fire and destructions to obtain even a negative accordance of the text with the existing buildings, but even this will not get over the indication of the locality being opposite the old Jerusalem.

In addition to the direct testimony, we have negative evidence almost as conclusive, for it must be borne in mind that, at the time when Eusebius wrote, the ruins of the old city must have been infinitely more complete and distinguishable than at any later period. The walls were breached by Titus, but their foundations remained, and (as we know from what even now exists) the superstructure also, in many places. We also know that at least three of its great towers, with the intervening wall, were left by Titus, and must have existed in Constantine's time.

The public buildings, though in ruins, must all have been easily distinguishable, and the ruins of the houses in a stone-built town, as Jerusalem always was, must still have encumbered the ground wherever they had stood.

---

* The relative position of these buildings is shown in woodcut No. 17, p. 41.

If, after all the vicissitudes the city has undergone during the last 15 centuries, enough still remains of the old city to induce such men as Clarke, Schultz, Robinson, and others to assert that the present church is situated in what was, and always must have been, the middle of the city, how much more clear must this have been in the 4th century, before any rebuilding had taken place!

The men of that day had the Bible in their hands as well as we have; and if the site now strikes us as improbable, the difficulty must have struck them with ten times the force it does us. Assuming the tradition to have been lost or imperfect, it seems impossible that Constantine should have chosen a site so at variance with the narrative in the Gospels Assuming the tradition to be perfect, it must have been in accordance with what we read in the Bible, and is consequently fatal to the pretensions of the present church to represent the locality of the scenes of the Passion.

In the Itinerary of the Bordeaux Pilgrim we have another contemporary record of what was then being done at Jerusalem, but unfortunately so indistinct that it is impossible to make much of it. Those who adduce his evidence in favour of the present building, maintain that the Porta Neapolitana is the Damascus Gate, but without any authority for such an assumption beyond the fact of Nablous being north of Jerusalem. On the other hand, it seems more logical to believe that this was the gate of the New Jerusalem just alluded to, in which case his testimony is final in favour of the views I am now contending for.*

---

* Since the above was written, this question has been set at rest by the publication of an account of the Holy Places by a pilgrim contem-

We have no direct authority with regard to the holy
localities between the time of Constantine and Justinian,
but it would be difficult to fancy any more direct and conclusive testimony than the fact above mentioned, which no
one doubts, of the latter Emperor erecting his church "secus
porticum Salomonis;" not, as I have just pointed out, within
the limits of the "accursed Temple" of the Jews, but on the
only available spot outside it, still remaining unoccupied in
proximity with the sacred Christian localities. There seems
to be no doubt but that the vaults to the eastward of the
Temple area are the substructures which Procopius describes
as raised by Justinian in order to obtain a level plateau for
this church. If this be so, I defy any one to suggest a
reason why Justinian should have erected his building in
this locality except on my theory. Had the Sepulchre been
at that time where it now is, his Mary Church would have
occupied the site of one of the two bearing that name, which
exist in close proximity to the Crusaders' Sepulchre.

In the same age we have a curious piece of circumstantial
evidence which in any court of law would probably be considered final. A traveller, Antoninus Martyr, after describing the
Holy Places, adds,* " Near the altar (of the Church of Golgotha) is a crack or opening (crepatura) where if you place your
ear you hear the flowing of water; and if you throw in an
apple or anything which will swim, and go to Siloam, you

---

porary, or nearly so, with the Bordeaux anonymous. According to this
author, the Porta Neapolitana was
the gate of the new city, attached
to the Prætorium of Pilate; and
the churches of Golgotha and the
Anastasis were close at hand in the

positions assigned to them in the woodcut, p. 41. The passages referring
to these objects in the narrative of
the Bordeaux Pilgrim, as well as this
anonymous author, are quoted at
length in Appendices A and B.

* Antonini Martyris Iter., ch. xix.

E

will find it there." Now this connexion between the cisterns in the Haram area and the fountains of the Virgin and Siloam had long been suspected, but only recently established by the explorations of Dr. Barclay and Sig. Pierotti, and no such connexion exists between the localities on the opposite hill and these fountains. This, therefore, is one of those pieces of unconscious testimony which are so valuable in cases of this sort, where there can be no mistake and no motive, and which consequently ought to be considered final till some new fact gets rid of their "damning testimonies."

The next great event in the history of the sacred localities is the capture of the city by the Persians in 614, and the reported destruction of the Christian churches by fire at that time.

This fire has been as useful to the advocates of the present localities as that at Wolf's Crag was to Caleb Balderston, though it would be easy to show that the damage done by the Persian was about equal to that effected by the Scotch conflagration. In the first place, Eutychius,* who is the principal authority in this case, expressly says that two only of the churches were damaged by fire, "igne injecto," the two others only plundered. But the great proof is that a simple monk, named Modestus, restored the whole to their pristine magnificence, without means or money, at a time when the city was still at the mercy of the Persians, and its wretched inhabitants subsisting on the alms of the Egyptian Patriarch. And we find no further complaint of the damage done by the Persians, either at the Mahometan conquest twenty-three

---

* Eutychii Ann., vol. ii. p. 212.

years afterwards, or when Arculfus describes the four churches
as complete and perfect at the end of the same century in
which the Persian invasion took place.

The detailed narratives which we possess of the conquest
of Jerusalem by the Saracens let in a flood of light on the
matter we have in hand. On the day of the conquest, when
the hour of prayer arrived, Omar requested to be conducted
to the Mosque of David, that he might pray there, and the
Patriarch took him to the Basilica of Constantine, saying,
"This is the Temple of David." An expression he could not
have used were he speaking of buildings in the town, or the
present Sepulchre, but is not unnatural in referring to a
church so near the Temple as this was, supposing me to be
right in the localities I have pointed out. But Omar replied,
"Thou liest; this is not the place described to me by the
Prophet of God;" and refused to pray there.* He then
proceeded to the Gate of Mohammed,† a perfectly well-
known locality south of the Jews' Wailing-place, which
was then, as it is now, blocked up nearly to the lintel.
Here, creeping in on his hands and knees, he came at
last to a place where he could stand up, and exclaimed,
" God is great! By Him who holds my soul in his hands,
this is the Temple of David."

If we compare the discovery of an underground Sakhra with
Eusebius's description of the rock, " standing erect and alone
in a level space," we at once see how different the two things
are. The position of Omar's Rock is clearly marked out by
that of the Gate of Mohammed, and by other circumstances
in the narrative which prove incontestably that it was within

---

* Eutychii Ann., ii. p. 284. Jelal ed deen, p. 174 et seq. Fundgruben des
Orients, v. p. 160. † See woodcuts, pp. 19 and 41.

the substructures of the Temple. The only doubt that seems
possible is whether it was under the Holy of Holies, or under
the Altar of the Jews. My impression is that the latter is
indicated, though this can only be determined by future
researches.

What Omar built at Jerusalem was either the little mosque
overhanging the southern wall (woodcut No. 16), which still
bears his name, or a similar oratory, a little to the west of
this, which Abd el Malek afterwards incorporated in the
Aksah. The erection of the last-named building, between
the years 685 and 691, is described in all the minutest
details by the various Mahometan historians of that age,
but their writings do not contain one single word which can
be considered as descriptive of the Dome of the Rock.

The last author to whom time will admit of my alluding
here is Arculfus, the French Bishop, who visited Jerusalem
in the end of the seventh century, and described the Holy
Places with a minuteness of detail surpassing all other authors
of that epoch.

He not only describes the four churches of the Christians,
but gives a plan, a "vile figuration" as he modestly calls it,
which, if taken in conjunction with his text, enables us to
understand clearly what he means, and to prove incontestably
that he was not speaking of one church containing all the
localities under one roof as we now find them.*

First, he describes the Anastasis, or Round Church,
containing the Sepulchre. Secondly, the Square Church of
St. Mary. Third, another very large church on the east of
the Sepulchre ("pergrandis ecclesia orientem versus"), called

---

* Acta Sanct. Ord. Bened., sæc. iii. p. 484 et seq.

the Church of Golgotha. Fourth, the Basilica, or Martyrium, constructed by Constantine with great magnificence.

Between the Sepulchre and the Church of Golgotha was a large place, the dimensions of which we get from Antoninus, who says it measured 400 feet.* And in this, it is added by Arculfus, was the place where Abraham erected his altar for the purpose of slaying his son Isaac, a locality always, before the Crusades, connected with the vicinity of the Temple, and never supposed to have occurred in the town. If you compare this description with the localities as laid down on the diagram (woodcut No. 17, p. 41), every word is intelligible and accurate. If you attempt to apply it to the present localities in the town, not one syllable is either accurate or applicable.

Of course this is not all, and no doubt there are other paragraphs in the authors just quoted which may be assumed to have a different meaning, and some which are so general that they will apply to any church or building in the world; but as time will not admit of my quoting or explaining these, you must allow me to say that I have read every mediæval historian I could obtain a reference to, bearing on the subject. Not being an Arabic scholar, my studies in that direction have been confined to such writers as have been translated into the various European languages, but they are tolerably numerous, and are the most important. Beyond this, however, I may mention that Sir H. Rawlinson kindly placed his valuable library of Oriental MSS. at my disposal, and I employed a competent scholar to abstract and translate all those passages bearing on the subject.

Bear with me therefore when I state broadly that the

---

* Ant. Mart. Iter., ch. xix.

result of all this reading has been that I can honestly assert that, in so far as I am capable of giving an opinion on such a subject, the above is a fair abstract of the historical aspect of the subject, and that it fully bears out and confirms in every respect the conclusions derived from the architecture of the buildings in question.

Even if I might be permitted to assume that all this appears as clear and as conclusive to you as it does to me, I am aware of one objection which will arise in most of your minds, and which to many will seem an almost insuperable difficulty. You would like to ask me—You assert that Constantine built the Dome of the Rock over what he believed to be the Sepulchre of Christ, and it continued to be considered as such for at least five centuries: if this be so, how is it possible that the present church has been believed to contain the real tomb for the last eight centuries? How, in short,—when, and in what circumstances, did the transference take place? And how is it possible that no record of such a transaction can be adduced?

Before answering these questions I should like to condemn those who ask them to a month's reading of the 'Legenda Aurea,' or any other collection of monkish legends. If they did not go mad in the process, as many have in modern times, they would rise from the perusal with a distinct idea how utterly dark and benighted these ages were, and prepared to admit anything, however monstrous and incredible it may appear when judged by the light of the 19th century. To take one of the most notable instances. There are those among us who still believe that the Santa Casa was carried by angels from Nazareth to Loretto, but they are few; and probably all those I am now addressing look upon it as a monkish

legend, though the evidence, judged by itself, is complete
and irrecusable.   Those who believe in its transference from
Palestine to Italy can have no difficulty in believing that the
Sepulchre may have been transferred from one hill to the
other.   Those who refuse their adhesion to the miracle of
the Santa Casa ought to have no difficulty in believing that
those who fabricated the evidence in favour of the one transference were as capable of suppressing the evidence that
explained the other, more especially as the Italian transference, if it took place, was in fact a miracle of the most
pretentious kind,—the Jerusalem transference a mere matter
of every-day business.

In so far as the evidence at our disposal enables us to form
an opinion, the transference seems to have taken place
somewhat in the following manner.

Two or three centuries after the capture of the city the
Saracens had increased in power relatively to the Christians,
while the capitulation of Omar had fallen into desuetude, and
the Moslems then cast longing eyes on the Dome of the
Rock; either because they were offended that the Christians
should possess a more splendid building than themselves in
the immediate proximity of and in front of their Aksah, or it
may have been that they coveted the custody of the Tomb of
Christ, whom they look upon as the greatest of Prophets next
after Mahomet.

Whether it was from envy or desire that they coveted the
possession of this building, this at least is certain, that
difficulties about the Holy Sepulchre arose as early as the
time of Charlemagne, and, at all events, that in the beginning of the 11th century the Chalif El Hakim drove
the Christians not only from their Sepulchre but from

their city, destroyed their churches, and persecuted them with a savageness that led to the reaction of the Crusades.*

When in the middle of the 11th century the Christians timidly crept back to Jerusalem, what did they do? What, indeed, ought they to have done? but build themselves a church in their own quarter of the town, and build it in such a form as was suitable for the performance of the Easter rites.

There was no fraud in this, nor attempt even to deceive. Every important town in Europe in that age had its San Sepolcro, mostly circular in imitation of that at Jerusalem, and devoted to the same purpose. Every parish church had its Sepulchre, in which at Easter they simulated that the body of Christ was laid; not to deceive, but to excite devotional feelings by representing the presence of the Divinity.

All this was more necessary and more natural at Jerusalem than elsewhere, and was accordingly carried out more effectively.

In the 19th century we should have called for records and documents, and insisted on proofs of authenticity. In the 11th century their faith was simple and unquestioning. To men who could neither read nor write, and who knew as little of Jerusalem before they went there, as we know of Timbuctoo, one sepulchre in Jerusalem was as good as another, and equally excited their feelings of sorrowful devotion. They believed whatever their priests told them; and after a century of possession, it is by no means clear that the

---

* When I first wrote on this subject the balance of evidence appeared in favour of the 11th century as the date of the appropriation of the sacred Christian localities by the Moslems. Subsequent research and reflection induce me to fancy that possibly it may have been earlier.

priests themselves may not have come to believe, as they do now, that the localities they now point out really witnessed the scenes of the Passion.

To any one at all familiar with the literature of those dark ages all this must appear so usual and so natural that it can hardly prove a difficulty; but we are so apt to apply the science of our own age to that epoch when a wholly different state of affairs existed, that it is not every one who can realize how deep the darkness of that night of intellect really was, and how strange to our conception the things then done.

The exact epoch when the transference took place is more difficult to fix than the mode, but fortunately it is of infinitely less consequence. To take a familiar illustration. Suppose in 1850 you found a certain Mr. Smith carrying on business and living over his shop in Oxford Street, and in 1860 found the same person settled for like purposes in the Strand, you would feel certain that between those dates a transference had taken place. Whether in consequence of a bankruptcy, or because prosperity had rendered his former premises too small; whether it was in 1851 or 1852, or any other year, are matters that may be settled hereafter, and do not affect the real question at issue.

So in the present instance we may feel certain that, from the time of Constantine to that of Charlemagne, the Dome of the Rock was considered as the tomb of Christ. From the time of the Crusades, and for some years before then, the church in the town has been supposed to contain the sacred spot; and if this be so, a transference certainly took place between these epochs.

From the correspondence about the keys of the Sepulchre

between Charlemagne and Haroun al Rashid, we know that
difficulties had already arisen at that date; but whether
the transference took place then or at the time of El Hakim,
may be reserved for future investigation. The fact is all
that it is important here to contend for, and that seems in-
disputable.

I have reserved to the last the question which is the most
important of all, and which indeed is the only thing that renders the controversy worthy of the attention of learned men,
or which justifies me in bringing it before you this evening.
It is this—How far do the localities I have been pointing out
agree with the narratives of the Evangelists in describing the
circumstances of the Passion?

I have already pointed out to you that many earnest and
learned men, both Catholics and Protestants, have gone to
Jerusalem with the Bible in their hands, and have been forced
to admit that the localities at present pointed out do not
agree in any particular with the sacred narrative; but most of
them, when asked to point out where they consider the event
to have taken place, have been forced to confess, like Dr.
Robinson, that probably the Tomb of Christ must for ever
remain unknown.

Against this melancholy negative it may be boldly asserted
that the localities now pointed out do agree in all essential
particulars with the Bible narrative. In order, however, to
understand this, it is necessary to explain that the wall which
now bounds the Haram area on its eastern side was built by
Herod Agrippa twelve years after the Crucifixion.* Before
that time the area was open, and lay outside the town.

* Josephus, B. J. v. iv. 2.

The Turris Antonia, I believe, all admit was the Prætorium,
or residence of the Roman Governor.   And no one doubts
that it stood at the north-west angle of the Temple, near
where the Mekhmeh now stands.   Christ was led from this
"towards the country," to a spot called Golgotha,* on the
brow of Kedron, there crucified, and buried in a rock-cut
sepulchre nigh at hand, in a place where from several
incidental circumstances we know that tombs certainly
existed.† If you adopt the views I have been endeavouring
to lay before you, there is not one circumstance of the
Bible narrative which is not clear and natural.   If you
try to reconcile the localities now pointed out with the
books of the Evangelists, you are met with improbabilities,
not to say impossibilities, which no one has been able yet to
explain away, and which have induced many who wished to
believe to reject the tradition in toto, and to believe that
there is now no hope of ever reconciling the traditional topography of Jerusalem with the events of the Bible narrative.

For the first time an opportunity of doing this is afforded
by the views I have been explaining to you.   If they are
adopted, all is clear, and you may walk round the city with
the implicit conviction that at last you know, within a few
feet at least, the localities where the events of the Passion
took place.

If all this is so clear as here stated, it may well be asked

---

* There seems to be nothing in the
Bible to lead us to suppose that Golgotha was a hill, or even elevated
spot.   The "Monticulus Golgotha"
seems purely a creation of the mediæval authorities, and might consequently be urged as an argument
against the little shrine in the present
church, if it had not been discovered
that that is built up of loose boul-
ders, some of which at least are of
granite!   So that its being a sham
prevents its being used as an argument against itself.

† Josephus, B. J. v. vii. 3.   Ezekiel xliii. 8, 9.   Nehemiah iii. 16.

how comes it that no competent and impartial person has
taken the trouble to go into the question during the last four-
teen years, and give a clear judgment on the subject either
for or against? Is it that new truths, like new wine, are so
distasteful that they are unfit for use till they have ripened in
darkness for years? or is it that men do not feel any real
interest in the subject? It may very well be argued that our
faith is so strong that it does not require any local or topographical support. But is this wise, and does it apply to all?
Would it not be well that all could feel that even in the
minutest particulars the narrative of the Evangelists could be
shown to be now capable of proof? Would it not be well that
even the smallest vantage-ground should be taken from the
assailants?

Whatever others may think, I feel strongly that the question is worthy of the earnest attention of the best class of minds;
and I feel confident that whenever competent and impartial
men seriously turn their attention to the investigation of the
data I have so imperfectly laid before you, they must arrive
at the same conclusion as I have done, which is—that the
building at Jerusalem popularly known as the Mosque of
Omar is the identical building which Constantine erected
over what he believed to be the Sepulchre of Christ.

LECTURE

DELIVERED ON THE 3RD OF MARCH, 1865.

PART I.

INTRODUCTORY.

LADIES AND GENTLEMEN,

Three years ago I had the honour of laying before
you, from this place, certain views respecting the topography of Jerusalem, and the site of the Holy Sepulchre
in that city.

The arguments I then brought forward must have been
so new to most of you that I fear you can hardly have
followed them sufficiently in the short space of time allotted
to a lecture to be able to form a deliberate judgment on
the matter then submitted to you. I have, of course, no
means of knowing what impression the reasoning then
adduced made on your minds. But this I do know, that,
even if not conclusive in favour of the sites I then pointed
out, no refutation of my views has since that time been
put forward. There has, it is true, been a great blowing
of trumpets and of penny whistles—a good deal of anonymous misrepresentation, and skirmishing with the outposts
of the argument. Several feints have been made to dis-
tract attention from the real points at issue. But it cannot
be ascertained whether the citadel is really impregnable

or not till it is fairly and openly attacked, and this has
not yet been done, nor does any one seem inclined to
undertake the task of besieging it.   In the mean while,
however, there was one argument which was currently used
everywhere, and which answered almost every purpose
nearly as well as a regular refutation.   Whenever any
one, who was supposed to be an authority on the question,
was asked what he thought of my views, it was easy to
answer—"What can Mr. Fergusson know about the matter?
He has never been at Jerusalem!"   It was wonderful how
much trouble such an answer saved, and how conclusive it
was considered.   It was in vain that I contended then, and
repeat now, that going to Jerusalem had nothing whatever
to do with the question,—that all the data for forming an
opinion were available in this country; in fact, that it
was fairer and better that I should not go, because while
I stayed away I placed every one on the same level with
myself; every fact, every scrap of information on which I
had based my conclusions was as available to every one who
chose to look into the question as it had been to myself.
I could pretend to no exclusive information or advantage,
and consequently the refutation, if it was to come, must
have been final and conclusive, and would have left me
no loophole to escape.   Be this as it may, even that
answer is now unavailing.   I have been to Jerusalem.   I
have examined the disputed sites personally, and I have
come back hardly a wiser, even if a sadder, man.   In other
words, I have seen nothing on the spot to induce me to
alter, in any essential respect, the views I had the honour
of submitting to you on the former occasion, but a great
deal to confirm them.   If, consequently, I followed my own

inclination, I would repeat to you almost in the same words
the lecture I delivered here on the 21st February, 1862. I
will, however, spare you the infliction, and on the present
occasion I propose to take the argument backwards. I will
ask you to dismiss from your minds all the architectural
question on which I mainly insisted when I last addressed
you, and to follow me while I describe the appearance and
dimensions of the successive Temples of the Jews. If I can
convince you that the rock, which is situated in the centre of
the building popularly known as the Mosque of Omar, is, and
always was, known to be outside the Temple area, you will
be forced to admit that that building was not erected by
the Moslems—the only reason ever advanced by any one for
assigning it to them being that on that rock stood the Holy
of Holies, or the Altar of the Jews. If it was not built by
the Moslems, it was by the Christians; and if by them,
it could be no other than the church which Constantine
erected over what he believed to be the cave in which
the body of our Lord was laid, as I explained when I
last addressed you. The architecture is of his age, and
neither he, nor any other Christian, ever built a church
in Jerusalem, or anywhere else—the whole floor of which
was occupied by a great rock with a cave in it—but that
which Eusebius describes as the one erected by that
Emperor.

I have chosen this line of argument because I believe
that few of you have realized either the dimensions or
the form of the Jewish Temple. Still that building is so
frequently before your thoughts, and its name so frequently
passes your lips, that I hope to interest you while I detail
its dimensions, which I believe I can do with absolute

certainty, and describe its appearance, which I fancy I can also do with proximate correctness.

Before, however, proceeding to this branch of the subject, allow me to recapitulate as briefly as I can what I said on the last occasion. It seems desirable that I should do so, because many are present here to-night who did not hear what was then said, and some of those then present may perhaps have forgotten some of the arguments then put forward.

On that occasion I commenced by calling your attention to the fact that the present Church of the Holy Sepulchre is situated in the middle of the town, and that its locality was altogether so much at variance with the incidents of the Passion as recorded by the Evangelists that many pious and learned men had denied that it could possibly contain the tomb in which the Saviour was laid, notwithstanding the traditions which cling to it, and their inability to suggest any alternative.

I then explained how my attention had first been directed to the building popularly known as the Mosque of Omar. First, because it certainly was not a mosque, though so called, because it had no kibleh; but, on the contrary, its principal entrance was towards Mecca. Secondly, because, though architecturally a tomb in all its essential elements, there was no tradition of any one having been buried in it; and it was so splendid a monument, and of so recent a date, that it seemed impossible the tradition could have been so completely lost.

I then narrated to you how I obtained access to Mr. Catherwood's drawings of the interior of the building, and how the mystery was at once solved by the discovery that the architecture of the building was of the age of Constantine; and then, looking at the form of the building, the rock and its cave, and all the circumstances of the case, it appeared to me, as clear as the light of the sun at noonday, that it could not be anything else than the church which Constantine erected over what he believed to be the Holy Sepulchre.

A good deal of what I said on that occasion was devoted to explaining the cogency of the architectural evidence so adduced. If the case had been Gothic it would have been final, no one would have disputed it; but because the architecture of the 4th century had not been generally investigated with the same care, it was necessary to explain it more in detail.

I next showed that the Golden Gateway was a festal portal of the same age as the Dome of the Rock, and could not be anything but the gateway leading to the Court of Constantine's Basilica, as described by Eusebius, and then that the Mosque el Aksah was a Saracenic building of the end of the 7th century, and so much more modern in style, and so different in every respect from the other two, as to prove that they could not have been erected in the same age or for the same purposes, but that the two former must, at least, be some centuries earlier in date.

I then proceeded to explain the historical argument, which, so far as I could understand it, entirely confirmed the conclusions arrived at from the architectural evidence; but as I shall have to go over the ground again to-night, it is needless to say more about it now.

And, lastly, I pointed out to you how completely the localities now assigned to the events of the Passion accorded

with the Scripture narrative, and how impossible it had
been found by others to reconcile the localities pointed to
in Jerusalem with the facts as narrated in the Bible.

The question which I feel sure you must now wish to
address to me is—"How far did your personal experience
at Jerusalem confirm or alter these views?" The answer
is contained in the assertion I made when I last had the
honour of addressing you. It is, that the materials available in this country are ample for determining a question
of this sort. Catherwood's plans, Arundale's drawings, the
numerous photographs, and, I may now add, De Vogüé's
beautiful illustrations, since published, afford all the information required, and nothing that is new and important is
to be learned on the spot.

The one thing I was least prepared for was the extreme
beauty of the interior of the building. I remember perfectly the effect of the Taj Mahal, and the other great
Imperial tombs of Agra and Delhi, and I am tolerably
familiar with most of the tombs and tomb-like buildings
in other countries. But so far as my knowledge extends,
the Dome of the Rock surpasses them all. The architect
seems perfectly to have realised the instructions of Constantine when he desired that "this church should surpass
all others in beauty, and that the details of the building
may be such that the finest structure in any city of the
Empire may be excelled by this." There is an elegance
of proportion and an appropriateness of detail which does
not exist to the same extent in any other building I am
acquainted with. Its mosaics are complete and beautiful

in design, and its painted glass, though comparatively
modern (16th century), is more beautiful than any in this
country. These, combined with the mystery of the Great
Rock, occupying the whole floor of the sanctuary, make
up a whole, so far as I know, unrivalled in this world.
If the Mahometans ever achieved anything as beautiful
in any age or any country, the memory of it has passed
away. If ever they built anything resembling it, the
record of it is gone.

On the present occasion I had purposely gone to Jerusalem
via Constantinople. I spent ten days in that city studying
the buildings of Theodosius and Justinian, and of subsequent
ages, for, unfortunately, not one vestige exists there that can be
ascribed to the age of Constantine. Within three weeks from
the time when I had stood under the Dome of Sta. Sophia I
was comparing its architecture with that of the buildings at
Jerusalem. With my eyes full of the impressions received
from the buildings at Byzantium, and my memory fresh from
the study of all the ancient forms of architecture in that
capital, I was able to bring that experience to bear on the
buildings to which I have just been alluding. I went thence
to Cairo, and again cast my eye over what remains of its early
Saracenic buildings. The result of all this investigation was
that I could not trace one vestige in the architecture of the
Dome of the Rock of the style of Justinian's age or of anything that followed it. On the contrary, everything I saw at
Constantinople, or at Cairo, or in Palestine, served only to
confirm me more and more in the impression I previously
expressed, that the building commonly known as the Mosque
of Omar was erected in the 4th century of our era, and
could not have been erected either before or after that epoch.

At the same time the impression it left on my mind was that it worthily represented the last dying effort of the gorgeous but formal style of Pagan Rome, and realized the first effort of that Christian freedom and grace which afterwards culminated in our cathedrals.

There was one point, however, on which I hoped my journey to Jerusalem might enable me to throw some new light, but in this I was disappointed. De Vogüé, in one of his plates of the Dome of the Rock, has drawn a cross on the abacus of one of the capitals of the pillars of the building.

I felt convinced there must be more. On examination, however, I found that the knobs where they should have been had all either been chiselled off or plastered over. Personally, I feel certain they once were there, but I cannot ask others to be content with such negative evidence, and, indeed, in so far as any argument is concerned, one is as good as a hundred. No Christian buildings had been destroyed before this one is said to have been built, from which it could have been taken as suggested; and if it had, the Moslems certainly would have taken a hammer and knocked off the hated symbol before

[No. 18.] Capital in Dome of Rock. From De Vogüé.

putting it up, though they may negligently have allowed it to remain when once there.*

This, however, was not the worst of the case. As I explained to you before, when the earliest Christian architects were trying to get rid of the inconvenient and hampering entablature of the Romans, they first threw away the architrave, and used only a block to represent it over each pillar. This block (*Dossert*, the French call it) is almost universal in all the churches erected between the ages of Constantine and Justinian. It is not found before the first; it is very rare after the time of the last-named Emperor. But what is more to our purpose is this,—that during this epoch there is hardly an instance, when the block is used, where it is not adorned with the Labarum or Christian monogram (vide ante, woodcut No. 8, p. 22). De Vogüé is convinced that this emblem existed on the architrave blocks of the Golden Gateway, though partially obliterated, and I am convinced he is correct in this assertion.† Now all the pillars in the aisle at Jerusalem have this block, and I felt convinced that, if carefully examined, I should find the cross within the circle on each of their faces. I expected to find it chiselled off, but at Sta. Sophia, where all those within reach have been so treated,

---

* De Vogüé represents the capital in plate xx. of his beautiful work, and in p. 67 of his text he gives a curious cut of one of the capitals in the Basilica at Bethlehem, which he adduces as an example of the style of the age of Constantine. No one can look at the two drawings without seeing that the capitals belong to the same age, and possess the cross in similar position. If both are *in situ*, this settles the question. De Vogüé, however, insinuates that, though the Bethlehem capital is, that at Jerusalem is not. My inspection leads me to the opposite conclusion in so far as the last-named example is concerned.

† Vide ante, foot-note, p. 34.

it is easy to detect the former existence of the Labarum by the roughness of the surface which still shows its outline.

To my dismay I found that every architrave block had been covered up on all its four sides with slabs of marble, and not one had fallen away. The very presence of this elaborate mode of concealing it convinced me that the Labarum is there, but I cannot ask you to listen to such an argument.

Time will only admit of my alluding to one other point. Before I went to Jerusalem my attention had been called to an inscription in Cufic characters which runs round the whole of the interior of the building as a frieze, and which was supposed to be fatal to my views—for this reason: one short paragraph in it is said to contain the name and date of the builder. The date is 72 Hejira (A.D. 691); the name is Al Mamoun (A.D. 813-833). De Vogüé says the name is a forgery. It may as well be the date. At all events it is quite certain that this part of the inscription has been altered and falsified at some time or other, and consequently no argument can be based upon it. It may be the date or the name, but in either case it is only a mosaic inscription which may be of any date, and inscriptions have lied before now.* But the curious part of the business is, that the whole of the rest of the inscription refers to "Jesus the son of Maria," and to Him only, and His name is mentioned four times over in the inscription. Not one word about David or Solomon, nor of Mahomet, whom they now fable ascended from this rock on his night journey to heaven. If they believed that the rock was the site of the Temple or the Altar of the Jews, it seems impossible that allusion to that circumstance should be

---

* The inscription, as translated by De Vogüé, Temple de Jérusalem, p. 85, is given in Appendix C.

omitted. If they did not know that Christ was buried there, why should they take such pains to proclaim His mission on the walls? It might be suggested that it was because Jesus had prayed in the Temple; but even this, if probable in itself, will not hold good, because the place where Jesus prayed in the Temple is pointed out to this day, and according to Mahometan tradition was always pointed out, in the Mosque el Aksah to the west of the pulpit.

My conviction is that, whenever this inscription was put there, or by whomsoever it was compiled, its authors knew perfectly well that the building in which it was placed was one which had been erected in honour of Christ, and they meant to proclaim that fact to their co-religionists. By quoting the paragraphs from the Koran, they established their title to its possession as against the Christians. Though subsequently another tradition has attached itself to the building, yet when that inscription was placed there it was known to be the Sepulchre of Christ.*

Another curious question arises with regard to this inscription. The Dome of the Rock, or Templum Domini, was used as the patriarchal church of Jerusalem during the whole of the Latin Empire, and considered as sacred, or more so, than the Sepulchrum Domini, or present Church of the Holy Sepulchre. The Crusaders probably were bad Arabic scholars, but many of the inhabitants of Jerusalem could read it correctly. Now, is it likely that they would have

---

* A curious instance of the respect in which the Mahometans, after the crusades, held the Christian localities, occurs in the travels of Ricoldus de Monte Crucis, who visited Jerusalem about the end of the 13th century. Describing the Valley of Jehoshaphat, he adds—"Inde intravimus in sepulchrum pulcherrimum Virginis quod Saraceni cum multis luminaribus, et magnâ reverentiâ custodiunt."

allowed such an inscription—about the most prominent ornament of the building—to exist in the writing of the hated
infidel, and containing an absolute denial of the divinity
of Christ, of His being the Son of God, or of the possibility of a Trinity—"Praise be to God; He has no Son;"
"He does not share the empire of the universe;" "Jesus
is the son of Mary, sent by God and His word." "Do
not say there is a Trinity in God." "He is one; how
should He have a Son?" &c. Would the Crusaders have
allowed such sentiments as these to remain?

Notwithstanding the evidence of the Cufic character of the
writing, I cannot help fancying the whole is of the time of
Saladin.* But this is a point regarding which others are more
competent to judge than I am. All I wish to point out here
is the fact of the great Saracenic inscription of the building
being wholly devoted to the honour of Jesus the Son of
Maria. If it does not absolutely prove that those who placed
it there—whenever that was—knew the original destination
of the building, it is the most extraordinary coincidence I
am acquainted with. When we recollect how fervently the
Moslems reverence the Tombs of Abraham, Isaac, and Jacob,
at Hebron, and how sacredly they have guarded the Tomb

---

* When Saladin (A.D. 1176) recovered this building from the Crusaders, his first care was to pull down
the great cross which adorned its
summit; his next, to clear the rock
from the marble casing and ornaments
which the Crusaders had heaped upon
it. Then after various lustrations
Mahommed ben Zeky ascended the
pulpit and preached a sermon practically on the texts contained in this
inscription.

This oration is found at length
translated in Michaud, Hist. des Croi-
sades, vol. ii. p. 485.

The question is, Was that text selected because it was already written
on the walls; or was it put there in
consequence of having been used on
this occasion? Judging the transaction by itself, it would appear that
preaching the sermon and emblazon-
ing the text are parts of one and the
same transaction.

of St. John at Damascus, and how rigidly they have excluded Christians from visiting it, we should not be surprised at their desire to possess the Tomb of Christ, whom they look upon as only second to Mahomet, nor that they should since have prevented his disciples from gaining access to its sacred precincts.

I am not myself competent to give an opinion with regard to the age of this Cufic writing, but I am informed by those who have the requisite knowledge that such Cufic characters were used for sacred or monumental or numismatic purposes long after the date of Saladin.

This I do know, that in the monuments of Delhi we have abundance of Cufic writing which very much resembles this, and the earliest inscriptions of the Mahometans in India must be subsequent to 1206 A.D.*

The subject is a tempting one, and I would like to point out to you some minor peculiarities in the Aksah and Golden Gateway, but they are of little importance to the argument; and time warns me to proceed to the second branch of my subject.

---

* Since the above was written, the publication of the book 'De Locis Sanctis,' by Theodericus, edited by Dr. Titus Tobler, has throw a new light on the subject. He gives in detail the Latin inscriptions which adorned the walls of the building when he visited it, A.D. 1172.

It seems quite impossible to believe that the Latin and Arabic inscriptions could exist simultaneously in the same building, and the latter must therefore have been added, as suggested above, in Saladin's time.

The description of the Dome of the Rock, as given by this author, is printed in Appendix D. His repeated assertion that it was erected by Constantine will be remarked, not that it is of any real value in itself, but as showing that even then the old tradition was occasionally coming to the surface.

PART II.

THE TEMPLE.

—◦◦—

IN approaching the second part of my subject, I must again apologise if I appear to offend by being too elementary, and telling you what you may have thought you knew as well beforehand. You of course have all read your Bibles. But reading the Bible is very much like going to Jerusalem. Hundreds go there and see nothing, and to see anything with profit requires thought and long previous preparation. So it is with the architectural portions of the Bible, which, allow me to remark before going further, are the only parts on which I pretend to offer an independent opinion. Few are aware, till they make the attempt, how difficult it is to restore a building from a mere verbal description, what patience and forbearance it requires to avoid putting diffi- culties aside, and to try again and again till all the pieces of the puzzle can be fitted into a consistent whole. The very first building I shall allude to is a remarkable in- stance of this. For in order to understand the Temple, it is necessary to begin with the Tabernacle, which was the type and model of all that succeeded.

Most of you are familiar with its form as usually repre- sented in our illustrated Bibles and Bible Dictionaries. It is represented as an oblong box, square in section, and with the curtains thrown over it, as a pall is over a coffin. The first objection to this is, that it cannot be made to accord with the description in the Book of Exodus; but

even a more striking one is, that it is not a practicable
building. It is impossible to stretch curtains across a

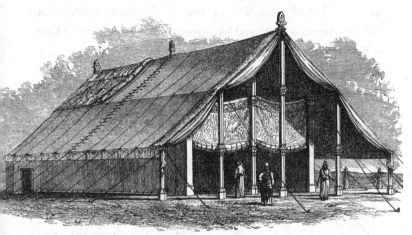

[No. 19.]   South-East View of the Tabernacle, as restored. From Smith's 'Dictionary of the Bible.'

space 15 feet wide without their sagging in the centre;
and every drop of rain that fell on the roof must pass
through, and the more skins or weight you heaped on it the
worse it would be.   But it may be suggested there is no rain
in these countries. The best information we possess on the
subject would lead us to believe that the rainfall at Jerusalem is considerably in excess of what it is in this country;
and as it all falls in the three winter months, the Tabernacle
would require more careful protection against rain in that
country than it would here. We do not know exactly what
the rainfall in the desert is, but there is no reason to suppose
it less than 30 inches nowadays, and it probably was more
3000 years ago.* Notwithstanding these objections, this
restoration has held its place for more than two centuries.

---

* Josephus (iii. 6, 4) mentions the linen vail which was used to protect
the front against snow.

Hundreds of thousands have accepted it without question, and hundreds have tried their hands at amending it without success. Yet the solution of the riddle seems easy. The Tabernacle was a tent; and like every tent from before the time of Moses to the present day, the tent had a ridge. Once this is suggested, the whole becomes clear. Every dimension of the Tabernacle is a multiple of 5, except the curtains, which were 14, because they were of course measured along the slope.*

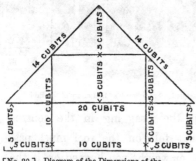

There were only four pillars in the interior, dividing the Holy Place from the Holy of Holies, but five in the porch, as there must be if there was a ridge. In fact, the moment you assume the ridge, which was indispensable as a protection against the weather, all the diffi-

[No. 20.]   Diagram of the Dimensions of the Tabernacle in Section.

culties disappear, and every part of the Bible description becomes intelligible. The dimensions of the Tabernacle in plan are given in such detail in the 26th and 36th chapters of the Book of Exodus, and repeated with so little variation by Josephus, Ant. iii. 6, that no difficulty has ever arisen with regard to them. The Holy of Holies was a cube of 10 cubits; the Holy Place, or pronaos, a double cube of the same dimensions. The one great mystery has been how to make the length of the curtains agree with this plan. When put together these measured 40 cubits by 28 for the under curtain; the upper one exceeded these dimensions

---

* The ridge of the roof was as nearly as may be a right angle, inasmuch as $10^2 + 10^2 = 14.14^2$.

by one cubit in length each way, so as to hang beyond it to
that extent on each side; and there were eleven breadths in the
upper curtain instead
of ten as in the lower,
so that when put to-
gether the upper hung
down 2 cubits at each
end. As the internal
dimensions of the build-
ing were only 30 cubits
by 10 cubits, unless you
assume a ridge, the cur-
tains were immensely
in excess of the dimen-
sions in plan.

Time will not ad-
mit of my going into
all the details of the restoration; but as they
have been published in
Smith's 'Dictionary of
the Bible,'* this is of
little consequence. I
will only add that
there are so many un-
expected coincidences in the account in the Pentateuch, that
it seems to me clear that it must have been written by some
one who had seen it standing. No one could have worked
it out in such detail without ocular demonstration of the
way the parts would fit together.

[No. 21.]   Plan of the Outer Court of the Tabernacle.

* 'Dictionary of the Bible,' vol. iii. p. 1451 et seq.

The dimensions of the Court are so clearly specified
(Exodus xxvii. 9 et seq), that fortunately there is no doubt
about them. It was a double square of 50 cubits. In the
outer half the altar and the laver were placed, in the inner
the Tabernacle itself. The whole was thus 100 cubits or
150 ft. east and west, by 50 cubits or 75 ft. north and
south.

TEMPLE OF SOLOMON.

THE great interest in a correct restoration of the Tabernacle for our present purposes arises from the fact that
it was the model on which the Temple was afterwards
constructed by Solomon.

A good deal of speculation has latterly prevailed as to
whether the Temple was copied from an Egyptian or an
Assyrian model. The former was in vogue thirty or fifty
years ago; but since Layard's discoveries the latter has been
the favourite theory. Now that we have got a correct
restoration of the Tabernacle, we are able to assert that
the Temple was not copied from either the one or the other.
According to the Book of Exodus, the plan of the Tabernacle was divinely revealed to Moses, and when it came
to be superseded by a more permanent structure it was
copied literally in plan and arrangement, with this singular
and marked distinction, that in the Temple every dimension of the Tabernacle was exactly doubled. Thus: —

The Holy of Holies in the Tabernacle was a cube of 10
cubits, in the Temple of 20.* The Holy Place in the Taber-

---

* The dimensions of the Taber-   iii. 6, 8; of the Temple, Ant. viii.
nacle are given by Josephus, Ant.   3, 2. Those of the Tabernacle are

nacle was a double cube of 10, in the Temple of 20 cubits. The porch of the Tabernacle was 5 cubits by 10, of the Temple 10 by 20. The verandah of the Tabernacle was 5 cubits wide, the chambers that surrounded the Temple measured 10. But perhaps the most remarkable coincidence is that the angle of the roof made the Tabernacle 15 cubits in height (woodcut No. 20), and consequently the Temple was raised by a false roof or upper chamber till its height was 30 cubits.*

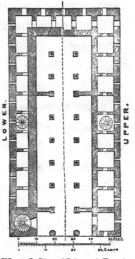

[No. 22.] Plan of Solomon's Temple, showing the disposition of the chambers in two stories.

Unfortunately the dimensions of the court of Solomon's House are not given either in the Bible or Josephus. But with the knowledge of this duplication before us, we may safely assume that the dimensions of the court of the Tabernacle were doubled also, and that the court of Solomon's Temple was in reality 100 cubits wide by 200 east and west, a dimension that we shall afterwards find fully confirmed by subsequent statements.

Before, however, proceeding to them, let me say a few words with regard to the cubit employed in these admeasurements. The Jews, according to the Rabbis, first used a small cubit of 15 inches, and applied it principally to the vessels and the furniture of the Temple. They next used

---

not given in figures in the Pentateuch, but are obtained from the details of the boards, &c.; those of

the Temple are found 1 Kings vi., 2 Chronicles iii.

* 1 Kings vi. 2.

one of 18 inches,—the first-named with a hand-breadth
added; and lastly, after the Babylonish captivity, it is said
they employed the Babylonian cubit of 21 inches, but this
is by no means clear.

For our present purposes it is sufficient to know that for all
their Temple measurements they used the cubit of 18 inches,
and that only. We feel certain of this, because in the Pentateuch, in the Books of Kings or Chronicles, in Ezekiel and
Ezra, in Josephus or the Talmud, wherever they speak of the
same place, they use the same number of cubits, which could
not, of course, be the case if they were employing cubits of different lengths. Whatever theories we may form with regard
to Jewish cubits, we know for certainty that Hecateus
and Josephus were using the Greek cubit of 18 inches,
and consequently, when they speak of the Holy of Holies as
a cube of 20 cubits, the Holy Place as 20 by 40, the court
as 100 by 200, in exact accordance with the measures given
in the Bible or Talmud, we cannot escape the conviction
that the cubits used by the Greek and Jewish authors are
identical. It may be added that the measurement of the
foundations of Herod's Temple on the spot where it once
stood gives exactly 400 cubits of 18 inches each, in strict
accordance with the dicta of Josephus.

This will be clearer from an inspection of the accompany-
ing table, in which the principal dimensions of the various
temples are collected together. Those printed in the ordinary
type occur in the various authorities referred to; those in
smaller type are inferred from the context, but may be
looked upon as tolerably certain, though not so much so,
of course, as the others.

In order to give you an idea of the dimensions of Solo-

DIMENSIONS OF THE TEMPLES OF THE JEWS, IN CUBITS OF 18 INCHES EACH.

		Tabernacle of Moses.	Temple of Solomon.	Temple of Ezekiel.	Temple of Zerubbabel.	Temple of Herod according to Josephus.	Temple of Herod according to Talmud.
Holy of Holies	Length	10	20	20	20	20	20
	Width	10	20	20	20	20	20
	Height	10	20	20	20	20	20
Holy Place	Length	20	40	40	40	40	40
	Width	10	20	20	20	20	20
	Height	10	20	20	20	60	40
Porch	Depth	5	10	20	20	20	20
	Width	10	20	20	20	25	20
Verandah	Width	5	..	..	..	..	..
Chambers	Width	..	10	..	..	..	..
Chambers and Gallery	Width	..	..	20	20	20	20
Total	Length	40	80	100	100	100	100
	Width	20	40	60	60	60	60
	Height	15	30	60	60	100?	100?
Inner Courts	Length	50	100	100	100	100	100
	Breadth	50	100	100	100	137	137
Outer Courts	Length	100	200	300	300	400	500
	Breadth	50	100	100	100	400	500
Sanctuary	Length	..	..	3000	..	..	..
	Breadth	..	..	3000	..	..	..

G

mon's Temple, I may mention that the building itself was, as
nearly as may be, of the size of the church of St Paul's,
Covent Garden. If that building had a flat roof, and its
interior was occupied by two chambers surrounded by a range
of cells on three sides, it would, mechanically, very nearly
represent the most celebrated building in the world.

Most of our London churches, such for instance as St.
Martin's-in-the-Fields, are, both as to dimensions and lithic
ornament, larger and more splendid than Solomon's Temple.
The truth seems to be that it was built in the " Bronze Age "
of architecture, which, unlike what happened in archæology,
preceded the great " Stone Age." Its magnificence consisted
in the brazen pillars of its porch, its brazen seas and altars, its
cedar pillars covered with gold, and generally in its richness
and metallic splendour. Those employed to build it were
smiths, not masons, and consequently any attempt to compare it with our modern buildings is absurd, and, I am afraid,
every attempt to restore its features by drawing equally
hopeless. No specimen of the brazen architecture of those
days has been preserved, and no representation of it is known
to exist. So we must at least wait a little before we can hope
to realize the appearance of this celebrated building.

TEMPLE OF EZEKIEL.

THE Temple which comes next in point of time is that
which Ezekiel saw in a vision on the banks of the Chebar,
and which he described in the 40th, 41st, and 42nd chapters of his book. This has proved a greater stumblingblock

to commentators than the Tabernacle itself, and in order to restore it they have been obliged to apply cubits of different lengths, and, what is worse, to suggest that when the Prophet said reeds (the reed was a measure of 6 cubits or 9 feet) he meant cubits, and when he said cubits he meant reeds, &c. All this is of course absolutely inadmissible, but it has so confused the subject that I confess when I last wrote regarding it I was so lazy as to take for granted that the vision was inexplicable, and was induced to pass it by.   Still, when fairly grappled with, nothing can be plainer, in so far at least as all the main dimensions are concerned.   Our ignorance of the exact equivalent of many of the Hebrew architectural terms renders some of the details obscure, but for our pre-

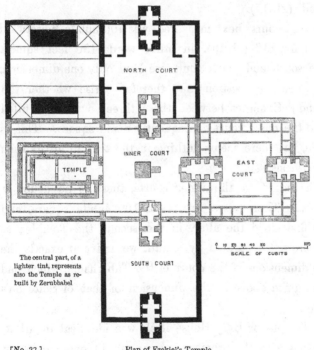

The central part, of a lighter tint, represents also the Temple as rebuilt by Zerubbabel

SCALE OF CUBITS

[No. 23.]   Plan of Ezekiel's Temple.

sent purposes at least these are unimportant and may be put aside for future investigation.

The prophet minutely describes in succession the six great gateways of the Temple—three belonging to the outer court or courts, and three to the inner court. The details of the arrangement of these edifices are a little difficult, and may be open to controversy, but their general dimensions are perfectly clear. They were 50 cubits in depth (75 feet), and 25 cubits (37 feet 6 inches) in width. One third seems to have been outside the wall, one-third projected into the court, and the middle was the width of the cloister, or range of chambers that surrounded the courts. The distance from the inner face of the one to the outer face of the next was 50 cubits (xl. 15).

The east court, next measured, was 100 cubits " eastward and northward" (xl. 19), in other words 150 feet square. Of the south and north courts we have only one dimension, 100 cubits. A question may therefore arise whether the N.E. and S.E. angles between these three courts were filled up, and the outer court consequently made square. This is possible, but there seems nothing in the text to justify such an hypothesis.

With regard to the inner courts, there is no doubt or difficulty. There were two, each 100 cubits square, and in the first stood the altar, in the second the Temple; as they were not separated by a wall, we arrive at exactly the double dimensions of the court of the Tabernacle, which had been assumed above as the dimension of that of Solomon's Temple.

The Temple or Holy House itself was identical in all its dimensions with the previous one, except in one particular.

In Solomon's Temple, the chambers, which surrounded it on three sides, were all thoroughfares, and, to gain the last, every one must have had to pass through all the previous ones. To remedy this inconvenience, in Ezekiel's Temple a passage was provided 5 cubits wide, with a wall 5 cubits thick. So that the width over all was increased from 40 to 60 cubits.

A new feature is also introduced—the range of priests' chambers, with the treasury and other appurtenances in the N.E. angle, between the Temple court and the north outer court. Its details cannot easily be made out, but its position and general dimensions are all that interest us just now. It may have existed attached to Solomon's Temple, though it is not mentioned, and in Herod's it was replaced by the Tower Antonia, occupying the same relative position, and used for the same purposes. (Ant. xv. ii. 4.)

So far all is not only clear, but minutely consistent with what we know was done both before and afterwards; now, however, we come to the great stumblingblock of restorers. At verse 15, chap. 42, it is said,—" Now, when he had made an end of measuring the inner house"—viz. the Temple proper— " he brought me forth toward the gate, whose prospect is toward the east, and he measured it round about, &c., 500 reeds," that is 4500 feet, or nearly an English mile, north, south, east, and west. Those who have hitherto tried to restore this Temple have felt themselves constrained either to contract this to the limits of a reasonable temple, or stretch the temple to these dimensions. Neither is possible nor required. This outer wall was only 9 feet high (xl. 5), and was the boundary, not of the *Temple*, but of the *Sanctuary*, a separation, as the Septuagint expresses it, " between the just and the unjust." It was, in fact, the first of the great measurements by which

Ezekiel divided the whole of Judæa, like the squares of a
chessboard, between the city, the priests, the princes, and the

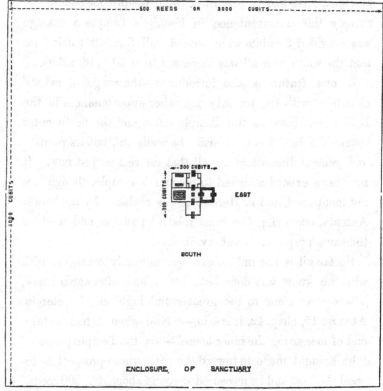

[No. 24.]   Plan of Ezekiel's Temple, with outer boundary wall.

Twelve Tribes of Israel, measurements which had and could
have no topographical existence, but were a geometrical expression of the relative importance of the different allottees.

This becomes even more strikingly evident when we turn
to the 45th chapter, where the prophet again mentions the
measurement of 500 reeds square for the Sanctuary, when
speaking of the division of the land only, without reference
to the Temple and its dimensions.

The truth seems to be, when closely looked into, that these figures only represent one of those simple arithmetical ratios to which the Jews were always so partial in architectural matters.

The Temple, as we have just seen, was 300 cubits (450 feet) east and west, as well as north and south. The enclosure of the Sanctuary was ten times that amount, or 3000 cubits (4500 feet) square. In this respect it is an exact counterpart of all the other measurements of the land of Israel found in Ezekiel's vision.

It is important, however, to point this out, because in after times the Rabbis adopted 500 as the sacred measure of the Temple, slurring over the fact that the prophet spoke of 500 reeds of nine feet each, not cubits of eighteen inches, though this makes all the difference. Notwithstanding this, they insisted upon this number in spite of local discrepancies, and all the difficulties which such an arbitrary determination necessarily introduced. It is the only essential point, as we shall presently see, in which Josephus and the Talmud are at variance.

If the Rabbis had taken the pains to add together the dimensions of the Temple, as given by Ezekiel, they would have found the result to have been 300, not 500 cubits; or if they had turned both into cubits or into feet, they would have found that the essential measurement was not 500, but 300 and 3000 cubits, or 450 and 4500 feet respectively. They would thus have saved future commentators a vast amount of trouble in trying to reconcile the measurements with the facts of the case.

TEMPLE OF ZERUBBABEL.

AFTER their return from captivity, the Jews rebuilt their Temple on the same site, and, as we learn from the Book of Esdras and Josephus,* with the same internal dimensions, as that before erected by Solomon. The one difference seems to have been that they adopted the passage to the chambers round the house as described by Ezekiel, thus making the total width 60 instead of 40 cubits, but the Temple itself, viz. the Holy of Holies, and the Holy Place, remained as before.

The porch, however, seems to have been increased in depth to the same extent as the external chambers, 20 cubits, instead of 10, as in Solomon's. The total dimensions of the House, with its chambers, therefore became 100 cubits by 60, instead of 80 by 40, as in the original Temple.

The size of the courts is not mentioned by our usual authorities, but fortunately Hecateus, of Abdera, visited Jerusalem in the time of Alexander, and tells us that this Temple was situated within a stone enclosure or wall measuring 100 cubits in width, and "about 500 feet" in length, or exactly the dimensions we obtain from the previous authorities. The north and south courts of Ezekiel—marked by a different tint on the plan, No. 23, p. 83—had not been built—only the two inner ones, and the outer east court. The width, 100 cubits, is the same as that mentioned by Ezekiel, and is the dimension assumed above for that of Solomon;

---

* Esdras vi. 3. Josephus, Ant., xi. 4, § 6.

and allowing for the thickness of the walls (36 feet) and
the projection of the gates, the expression "about 500 feet"
is as correct as could be desired.   In fact, if we cut off
from the plan of the Temple as described by Ezekiel, and
drawn woodcut No. 23, the north and south courts, leaving
only the parts which are hatched, we have a perfect representation of the plan of that one which was erected after
the return from the Captivity.   So far, therefore, we walk
with perfect certainty both as to the general dimensions
of the two first Temples of the Jews, and also as regards
the length of the cubit employed.

It is scarcely necessary to go over again in detail the
dimensions of this Temple, as these have been sufficiently
explained in speaking of that of Ezekiel, and are figured
in the plan, woodcut No. 23.

The story of these two Temples appears to be this.
During the Captivity the prophet placed on record the
sacred arrangements and dimensions of the Temple, as they
had been revealed to Moses and David, and had been carried
into execution by Solomon.   To these he added such minor
suggestions as subsequent experience may have shown to be
expedient, and described such additions as may have appeared to him requisite to complete the *beau idéal* of a perfect
Jewish Temple.

When the Jews returned from the Captivity, they carried out
this specification and these suggestions to as great an extent
as their means admitted, in no instance departing from
the sacred model thus delivered to them, and sanctioned by
the Divine authority.   Hecateus' measurements make it quite
clear that the three central courts were all they had the means
of accomplishing.   The north and south courts were never

attempted, and the Citadel Baris—which may have existed
from David's time—supplied the place of the more symme-
trical arrangements suggested by the prophet in the north-
west angle.

From the Book of the Maccabees and Josephus we gather
that this Citadel was attached to the north-west angle of
the Temple, occupying the relative position of the treasury
and priests' chambers described by Ezekiel. It was afterwards pulled down by Herod, and rebuilt as the Antonia,
probably because it encroached on the space required for his
enlargement of the Temple, when it became necessary to
remove it further north. It still apparently encroached a
little on the area of the Temple at the angle; for we learn
from Josephus (B. J. vi. 6, § 4) that a prophecy existed that,
when their Temple became four square by the destruction
of the Antonia, their city should be taken. The prophecy
is, of course, of no value; but it seems to point out that
the Citadel was an integral part of the Temple, and projected into its area; otherwise it is hard to understand how
the Temple could become square by its destruction.

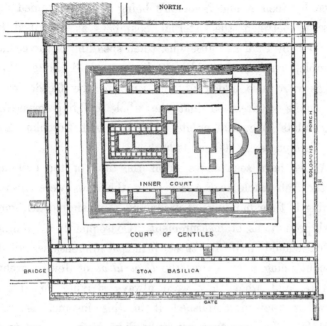

NORTH.

SOLOMONS PORCH

INNER COURT

COURT OF GENTILES

BRIDGE   STOA   BASILICA

GATE

[No. 25.]   Temple of Herod restored.   Scale of 200 ft. to 1 in.

HEROD'S TEMPLE.

WE now come to the Temple as restored by Herod, which
is by far the most interesting of all: first, because of its
greater architectural magnificence; but more than this,
because it was the Temple in which the ministrations of
our Lord took place, and also because it is the one
of which the foundations can still be traced out, and thus
becomes the turning-point of all topographical inquiries at
Jerusalem.

The House itself was only repaired. It was still standing
as rebuilt by Zerubbabel when Herod undertook its restoration, and the dimensions were not altered; the only differ-

ence between it and Solomon's being that it retained the passage between the external chambers as described by Ezekiel, by Ezra and Josephus, when speaking of the earlier Temple, making the width 60 instead of 40 cubits. Two wings were also added at this time to the façade, each 20 cubits square,* so that the whole building measured 100 cubits long, 100 cubits wide, and both Josephus and the Talmud assert 100 cubits high.

As we have seen above, from the time of the building of the Tabernacle to the last hour, the Jews were always aiming in their buildings at producing some simple arithmetical proportions of measurement. Consequently a building which should have its three principal dimensions equal, without being a cube, was the *beau idéal* of Jewish architecture, and what they were always striving to attain. Whether they accomplished it in this instance is still doubtful. In plan they certainly did; but if it attained the height of 100 cubits, it could hardly have been otherwise than by carrying up the wings so as to form two towers like those of York Cathedral; and to say the least of it, this seems very doubtful. It is safer to assume that in this, as in most other instances, Josephus, though always correct in plan, systematically exaggerates the heights.†

Be this as it may, it is evident that a building which was

---

* Josephus, B. J. v. 5, § 4.

† It may assist you in forming some idea not only of the dimensions of this building, but also of its form, if you compare it with the nave and façade of Lincoln Cathedral. To make this complete, however, you must fancy the side aisles divided into three stories of chambers by floors, and the clerestory also excluded by a floor from the nave. The height and width of the façade approximate very closely to those of the Jewish Temple; but if it is insisted that Josephus's height must also be adopted, you must adopt also the western towers, which I certainly would feel inclined to reject.

100 cubits wide could not stand in a courtyard of the same dimensions, and allow a passage round it. We consequently find the breadth of the inner court increased from 100 to 135 cubits or 202 feet 6 inches, while its length between the porticoes was 187 or 280 feet, leaving 20 feet for the cloisters, and the thickness of the walls.* The court was strongly fortified, having three gates on the north and three on the south side, and one—the most magnificent of all—towards the east—the Beautiful Gate of the New Testament, the Porta Speciosa of the writers of the 4th and 5th centuries.

What in the previous Temple had been the outer court, or Court of the Gentiles, was, in this one, cut in two, and appropriated to the women: its breadth was 135 cubits, as that of the great court; its depth is not given by Josephus, but the Talmud calls it 135—a mistake which has evidently arisen from their having adopted Ezekiel's number of 500 for the whole area, instead of 400 cubits, as Josephus tells us,† and as we know, from the existing remains in the ground, was the true measurement. In consequence, not knowing what to do with the 100 cubits they had to spare, they assigned them to this court. It is impossible, however, to suppose that, while the Court of Israel and the Court of the Priests measured each, only 11 cubits by 135, a space would have been devoted to the Court of the Women (a court which was an innovation and contained no object of interest) six times as large as these two put together, and nearly equal to the great court itself, which contained both the Temple and the altar, with its accompaniments. What its real dimensions

---

* These dimensions are from the Talmud (Middoth, ch. ii. sect. 6). They agree perfectly with those we arrive at from protracting Josephus's description.

† Josephus, Ant. xv. 11, § 3, and 9, xx. 10, § 7.

were we can fix with very tolerable accuracy by the protraction of the outer court. The Court of the Women was certainly either 35 or 40 cubits east and west, or within 5 cubits of that dimension, and 135 north and south.

So far all this was merely a repair and remodelling of the old Temple, larger and more ornate than the one it superseded; what Herod really added was the outer court, or Court of the Gentiles, which was required by the more cosmopolite policy of the Roman epoch. Josephus tells us he doubled the area of the Temple.* In fact, he increased it nearly five fold,† and the area of his Court of the Gentiles was as nearly as may be equal to the area of the portion appropriated exclusively to the Jews, or 180,000 feet.‡ In

---

* B. J., i. 21, § 1.

† The Temple, in the time of Alexander, as we learn from Hecateus, was 500 feet × 150 = 75,000; that of Herod was 600 × 600 = 360,000.

‡ As in every case of this sort, the real difficulty of the argument is not so much to prove which is right as to get rid of daring assertions or inconsequential logic on the part of opponents. When these are made by persons having authority, or who are entitled to respect either from their position or learning, they are too generally accepted without question. It is so much more convenient to believe than to inquire, so much easier to follow than to lead, that few care to adopt the contrary line of argument, and truth consequently must wait till somebody will patronize and chaperone her.

One of the more remarkable instances of this is to be found in the Count de Vogüé's recent work on the Temple of Jerusalem. The Count is

a scholar and a gentleman, and has had every opportunity of ascertaining the fact on the spot, and is quite above the slightest breath of suspicion that he would state anything which he had not convinced himself was quite correct. Yet between pages 16 and 21 of his work we find the following extraordinary comment.

He first fully and fairly describes the views and credibility of Josephus; and after giving him credit for general correctness, states that he makes the Temple four square, 400 cubits each way, and with the Antonia allows a total circumference of 6 stadia, 3600 feet. He then discusses the Talmud, which he admits also makes the Temple square, but 500 cubits each way, without mentioning the Antonia. Of course it would be easy to show from Josephus's account of the siege that the Antonia did not cover the whole of the width of the Temple, but that is of no consequence. Taking it as De Vogüé states it, the Temple was

this sense he may be said to have doubled it exactly. In other words, he appropriated an additional space to the Gentiles exactly equal to that belonging to the Jews.

The great glory of this outer court was the Stoa Basilica, or Royal Porch. It was 600 feet long, 100 wide, supported by 162 Corinthian columns, which divided it into three aisles, the centre one of which was 100 feet high.

It may assist you in forming some idea of this if you will fancy the transepts taken off the sides of York Cathedral, and added to the ends. In plan and section you will have a building whose dimensions are almost identical with this porch.

There were double porticoes surrounding the other three sides, but less in height, and of inferior magnificence, to the great Stoa Basilica, which, being situated at the end of the bridge which crossed the Tyropœon valley, always must have formed the principal entrance to the Temple from the city and the palace on the opposite hill.

To all this magnificence you must add the wonderful masonry of the terrace-wall, which we still see at the Jews' Wailing-place in the west, and in the southern wall under the Mosque el Aksah.

I do not know what impression these dimensions make

---

600 feet square, Antonia the same: the two together 1200 feet by 600. Having stated all this, and admitted that there are no other authorities on the subject, he then arrives at the astounding *non sequitur* that the Temple was an irregular parallelogram 1500 feet north and south, with an average breadth of about 1000, and a circumference of 1525 mètres, or more than 5700 feet, *exclusive* of the Antonia, instead of the 2400 of Josephus or 3000 of the Talmud, if we take even that extreme measure.

Of course no reasoning founded on such a basis can for one moment be admitted; but such is the authority of the Count, and so little are people disposed to look into such matters and judge for themselves, that it will no doubt be frequently quoted against the views propounded in the text.

on you.   Perhaps some of you are disappointed.   But
recollect, no temple of ancient times, out of Egypt, surpassed them.   The great temple at Palmyra covered about
the same area, but was far less magnificent.   That of
Baalbec was smaller, though, if ever completed, it would
have rivalled its splendours.   All those of Greece or Rome
covered a smaller area, and none were equal in magnificence.

In order to try and realise the whole, fancy a building
like the nave of Lincoln, raised on a lofty terrace, and
standing in a court surrounded by cloisters and porches.
Fancy these courts approached by ten great gateways,
each in itself a work of great magnificence; and again
this group surrounded by another court on a lower level,
one side of which is occupied by a building longer and higher
than York Cathedral, and the other three sides by cloisters
more magnificent than any we know of; and all this supported by terrace-walls of such magnificence of masonry,
that even at this day, in their ruined state, they affect
the traveller as much, perhaps, as any building of the
ancient world.

In the view of the Temple, forming the frontispiece, I
have attempted to realize, as nearly as may be, the general
features of this celebrated edifice.   I cannot now attempt to
explain the data on which this restoration is founded, but,
generally, I may say that I have taken a series of Asiatic
buildings, beginning with Persepolis, 500 years before Herod's
time, and ending with the Tâk Kesra, 500 years after it,
and, throwing into this that amount of Roman design which
must have prevailed at that period, I fancy the result must
have been something not unlike what is here represented.

The general arrangements and features are certain, and the details could hardly be very different.

The design of Herod's Temple may have wanted something of that classical simplicity we so much admire in other buildings of an earlier period, and its details may have been more gorgeous than pure.   But take it all in all, so complex a building, rising terrace above terrace, and court within court, must have afforded a variety of perspective and a splendour of effect which, coupled with its dimensions, must have equalled if it did not surpass anything we know of elsewhere.

PART III.

LOCAL INDICATIONS.

THE next point in such an inquiry as this is to ascertain how far these historical deductions are borne out by the indications on the spot.   In the present instance nothing can well be more satisfactory than their accordance.

In the first place, no one, I believe, doubts but that the south-western angle of the Haram enclosure is one of the angles of the Temple area.   The remains of the bridge across the Tyropœon, which is coincident with the centre of the "Stoa Basilica;" the gateway under the Aksah, which is certainly the double portal near the southern court mentioned by Josephus ;* the Gate of Mohammed, one of those mentioned by Josephus as leading to Parbar ;† and the

---

* Ant. xv. ii. § 5.   † *Loc. cit.*

general appearance of the masonry, all confirm this so completely that it seems impossible to doubt it.

If then we measure 600 feet eastward from this angle, all is practically solid up to that point. Indeed, the living rock can be seen on the surface over the greater part of the Haram area, and in other places can be traced in the underground cisterns extending under the Aksah, and approaching at least within a few feet of the surface. Beyond these 600 feet we come to a range of vaults, unequally spaced, badly constructed, and evidently of much

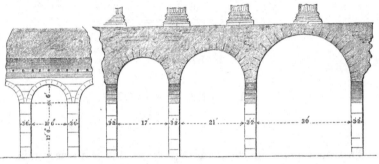

[No. 26.]   Section of vaults in S.E. angle of Haram, showing what would be the position of the pillars of the Stoa Basilica if it extended over them.

more modern age.* On these the Temple could not have been supported, so that, in this direction at least, the history and the topography are perfectly agreed.

Again, if we measure 600 feet northward from this angle, we come to a second bridge, one arch of which is said to have been discovered by Lieut. Wilson, at present surveying Jerusalem. According to such accounts as have reached home it is undoubtedly of Jewish—Herodian— masonry, and is situated exactly where we would expect to find it according to the accounts of Josephus. Between

* See plan of Haram Area, p. 41.

these two bridges the masonry of the terrace wall is of that splendid megalithic character which all ancient accounts would lead us to expect was employed in the substructions of the Temple, and which still exists on the south side, under the Mosque el Aksah. Between these two bridges Josephus tells us two gateways led down to the suburb Parbar (Ant. xvii. §5). One of these has been discovered, and is now known as the Gate of Mohammed; the other is probably hid by the buildings of the Mekhmeh.

But the most remarkable feature here is that portion of the wall known as the Jews' Wailing-place. If a line were drawn east and west through the Altar and the Holy of Holies, as

[No. 27.]   Jews' Wailing Place.

represented in woodcut No. 25, p. 91, it would cut the centre of the Wailing-place exactly, the dimensions of which are also, as nearly as may be, those of the rear of the Temple. This is too remarkable to be an accidental coincidence, and proves most distinctly that when the Jews selected it they knew perfectly well where their Temple had once stood, and what its real dimensions were.

The position of the great rock-cut reservoir in front of the Aksah — the watercourses, as far as they have been examined—all accord with such indications as are found in Josephus or the Talmud. With regard to the Temple itself the prophecy has only too literally been fulfilled; not one stone remains upon another, or anything which without our histories would enable us to fix its locality or dimensions with certainty. But its substructions still remain, and, with the assistance of Josephus and the Talmud, we may fix these with almost absolute certainty.

Every indication on the spot tends to show that the Temple of Herod was, as Josephus tells us, 400 cubits or 600 feet square, and was situated, as marked on the plan, No. 17, p. 41, in the south-western angle of the Haram area. Since, then, the rock, which now stands under the Dome of the Rock, is situated nearly 800 feet from the southern wall, it was certainly outside the area of the Temple, at a distance of 150 feet from its northern wall.

I need hardly stop to point out that this determination at once gets rid of all those theories which would place the altar of the Temple on the rock, even if their untenableness could not be easily demonstrated from other circumstances; and above all, it frees us from the incubus of Professor Willis's unsavoury suggestion, which would make the Bir Arrouah into a cesspool, and convert the Pool of the Virgin, the sacred fount of Siloam, and all that is poetic and beautiful in "the stream that flowed fast by the oracle of God," into so many reservoirs of liquid manure !* Over

---

* The chapters of the Talmud on which this strange theory rests (Middoth, ch. iii. secs. 2 and 3) have never been quoted by those who support it : had they been so, there would have been an end of the question at once,

these theories we need not now pause. Till it can first be shown that the rock was within the Temple precincts, they have no possibility of existence.

Before leaving this branch of the subject, it would be well to inquire where it is said that the altar of the Jews was placed on a rock. It certainly is not mentioned in the Bible, nor in Josephus, nor in the Talmud, nor in any other authority to which we usually apply on such occasions. What we know of the altar is that it was first of brass,[*] and then built up of small stones, on which no tool had been passed;[†] and as for its site, it was placed in the threshing-floor of Araunah. Now the rough rock beneath the Dome certainly never was nor ever could have been a threshing-floor. But besides this, we know that the site of the altar was lower than the floor of the Temple.[‡] If the altar had been placed on this rock, and the Temple erected between it and the Tyropœan Valley, its substructures must have been so gigantic that it is almost impossible they should have disappeared as they have done.

In fact, turn it which way you will, the Sakhra was not the site of the Jewish altar, and never could have been. 1st, It was outside the Temple area; 2nd, The Rock theory is a mere Mahometan tradition, which has been adopted without thinking; and lastly, there is no site for

---

irrespective of all local considerations. They are therefore printed in Appendix E, at the end of this volume.

There is one watercourse, discovered by Dr. Barclay, and marked on Pierotti's plan, running towards the south-west, which exactly accords with the description of the Talmud,

according to my restoration. The drain, which Pierotti and his friends rely upon, runs *northward* and *eastward*, or in the exactly opposite direction to the specification in the Talmud.

[*] 2 Chronicles iv. 1.

[†] Josephus, B. J. v. 5, § 6; Middoth, chap. iii. sec. 4.

[‡] Josephus, B. J. v. 5, § 4.

the Temple behind it, while every indication on the spot
contradicts such a hypothesis.

On the other hand, if we place the altar where shown
in the plans given above, and assign to the Temple the
limits and the site there shown, every local peculiarity
agrees with such a position, while every historical deduction
confirms the local indications.

Part IV.

H I S T O R Y.

There is still one point which requires to be alluded to
before the argument can be considered as complete. It
is this. Even if we assume it as quite certain that the
Temple was only 600 feet square, and that it was situated
in the south-west angle of the Haram area, and consequently
excluded the site of the Dome of the Rock from its precincts, still it may be argued that by the time of the
Mahometan invasion the knowledge of that fact was lost,
and the Moslems may have believed that the Temple extended very much farther north than it really did.

Fortunately, the proof that this was not the case is as clear
as that which has preceded, though, perhaps, not so easily
explained, inasmuch as the authorities on which the proof
rests must be, I fear, unfamiliar to most of you. In all
I have hitherto said I have been able to rely on your
knowledge of the Bible, or of the works of Josephus; but it
is different when I refer you to the Bordeaux Pilgrim, or to

Antonius or Arculfus, and still more so when I quote Jelal ed
deen or Mejr ed deen, or ask you to grub for information
in the 'Fundgruben des Orients.'   All I can promise,
therefore, is to be as brief as possible, and not to weary you
more than I can help with long or unfamiliar names.

Judging from what we now find at Palmyra, Baalbec, or
Gerash at the present day, it seems probable that a great
deal of the building of the Temple must have remained
standing three centuries after the capture of the city by
Titus. The Temple, it is true, was burnt, and its fortifications probably thrown down, at the end of the siege; but
how far its walls or its porticoes were destroyed we do
not know.

From the time of the siege we lose sight of the building
for near 300 years.   Incidentally we learn that Hadrian had
erected a temple to Jupiter on the spot, and the Bordeaux
Pilgrim* (A.D. 333) speaks of two statues of or by Hadrian
as standing there when he visited the place.   The same
authority speaks of the altar, the cisterns, and other accompaniments of the Temple as perfectly well known in his day,
and mentions the affecting custom of the Jews coming there
to weep over their lost sanctuary as they do now.

In the year 363 Julian commenced rebuilding the Temple,
and we cannot doubt but at that period the site and form
of it were perfectly well known.   We have the remains of
Julian's undoubted work in the doorway, underneath the
Aksah (woodcut No. 28), and some of the incidents of the
miraculous interruption to the attempt would lead us to
believe that there was then a church close at hand,† and

* See Appendix A.
† Gregory Nazianzen ad Jud. et Gent. 7. 1.   Sozomen.

that Julian's ambition was to rival the Christian church
which stood so near the spot. At all events it is quite

[No. 28.]   Frontispiece of Julian in south wall of Haram.

clear that the site of the Temple was perfectly well known
at that time.

"St. Jerome, about the year 400, notices an image of
Jupiter and an equestrian statue of Hadrian in the place of
the Holy of Holies; the gate of the Temple which led to
Siloam; and indeed the whole area of the Temple, in such a
manner as to leave no doubt that its position and limits, with
several of its leading features, were sufficiently marked in his
day." *

Aurelius Prudentius, writing in the beginning of the 5th

* Rev. Geo. Williams's 'Holy City,' vol. ii. p. 338, for which see references
to Jerome.

century, says, "Porta manet Templi, Speciosa quam vocita-
runt, egregium Salomonis opus" (Diptychon, xliv.). It
does not appear that the author visited Jerusalem himself,
but the fact must have been well known, or he would not
have asserted it so positively. His calling it a work of
Solomon proves that it was a gate of the Temple, not
of the city,—in fact, the Beautiful Gate opposite the door of
the Temple.

Antoninus, who wrote in the time of Justinian, adds very
little to our information regarding the Temple, though giving
such an admirable indication of the locality of the Holy
Places.* He mentions, however, this same Porta Speciosa,†
and says that its threshold and lintel were still standing. If
this were so, it is more than probable that some remains of
the more solid parts of the Temple were standing also; but
the position of the Beautiful Gate alone being known in
those days, made the centre line of the Temple equally
clear and certain.

From this period to the time of the Mahometan invasion,
A.D. 636, we have very little information on the subject;
but as the authors who relate that event are unfamiliar to
most of you, and the works that contain their narratives not
generally accessible, I shall quote the principal passages
entire, in order that you may judge for yourselves.

The first and best authority is Eutychius, the Patriarch

---

* Ante, p. 49.

† After the Mahometan conquest,
when this gate had disappeared, the
Golden Gateway appears sometimes
to have been called by this name,
but not at that age; nor will the
description in the text at all fit. The
words of the author are, " Porta Civi-
tatis quæ coheret Portæ Speciosæ,
quæ fuit Templi, cujus liminare
et trabulatio stat." (Itiner. Anton.
Martyr. xvii.). This gate was therefore then in ruins. The Golden Gateway is complete at the present day.

of Alexandria, who wrote about the year 870 A.D. He
writes as follows. On the terms being arranged, "the
gates were opened; and Omar entered the city and sat
with the Patriarch Sophronius* in the sacred place of the
Church of the Resurrection; and when the hour of prayer
was come, turning to Sophronius, the Chalif said, 'I desire
to pray:' to whom the Patriarch replied, 'Emperor of the
Faithful, pray where you now are;' but Omar replied, 'I
will not pray here.' He therefore led him to the Church
of Constantine, a mat being spread in the middle of the
church; but he still refused, saying, 'Nor will I pray
here;' but going out to the steps of the Church of the
Holy Constantine, which are on the front, looking towards the east, he prayed there alone on the steps." He
then gave his reasons for this proceeding, saying, that,
had he prayed within the church, the Moslems would, after
his death, have appropriated the place, because he had
prayed in it; and he even gave the Patriarch a writing, that
his praying on the steps should not be construed into a pre-
cedent. The narrative then proceeds: " 'Then,' said Omar,
'you still owe me one thing, according to the treaty (*fœderis
jure*); concede to me, therefore, a place where I may build
a temple.' To which the Patriarch replied, 'I give to the
Commander of the Faithful a place where he may build a
temple, which the Grecian Emperors were unable to build;†
viz., the rock on which God spoke to Jacob; which Jacob
called the Gate of Heaven; and the Israelites, the Holy of
Holies; which is in the middle of the earth, and was the Holy
Place of Israel, and is held by them in such veneration that,

---

* Eutychii Annales, vol. ii. p. 284.

† Alluding apparently to Julian's unsuccessful attempt.

wherever they are, they turn their faces towards it when they pray,—but on the condition that you give me a rescript that you will build no other place of prayer within Jerusalem, except this one;' which Omar having written, he delivered it to the Patriarch. For when the Romans embraced Christianity, and Helena, the mother of Constantine, built churches in Jerusalem, the place of the rock and those adjacent to it were laid waste, and so left; and they threw dirt on the rock, so that a large dunghill was heaped upon it, and the Romans did not reverence it as the Jews had done, nor did they erect any church upon it; because our Lord had said, in the Holy Gospel, 'Behold, your house shall be left unto you desolate;' and again, 'There shall not be left one stone upon another that shall not be cast down and laid waste.' On this account the Christians had left it lying waste, and had not erected any church upon it. The Patriarch Sophronius, having therefore taken Omar by the hand, led him to the dunghill, when Omar, taking his garment by the edge, filled it with the earth, which he threw into the valley of Gehenna."

The Mahometan historians tell nearly the same story, but with some slight variations. I shall quote that of Mejr ed Deen,* as the least generally accessible, and the parallel passage will easily be found in Jelal ed Deen.†

"When Omar had signed the treaty of peace, he told the Patriarch (or Patrician) to lead him to the Mosque of David. The Patriarch walked before them to guide them, and led them to the Church of the Sepulchre, and said, 'This is the Temple of David.' But Omar, having cast his eyes upon it

---

* Fundgruben des Orients, v. p. 160. † Jelal ed Deen, History of the Temple, p. 174 et seq.

and reflected a little, said, 'Thou liest! The Prophet of
God described to me the Temple of David, and it is not this.'
The Patriarch then conducted him to the Church of Sion,
saying again, 'This is the Temple of David.' Omar again
told him he lied. After which he conducted him to the
great church near the gate called the Gate of Mohammed.
Water ran down the steps of the gate, and ran out by the
street where the gate of the city was, in such a manner that
the greater part of the steps were below water. The governor
then said, 'We can only enter here by creeping.'—'Be it
so,' said Omar. Then those that were before Omar and
those that were behind him commenced creeping, till they
came to a plain place. Omar, having looked to the right
and to the left, exclaimed, 'God is great! By Him who
holds my soul in his hands, this is the Temple of David,
from which the Prophet told me he had made the night
journey.'

"They found there the rock Sakrah, covered with dung,
which the Greeks had thrown there in contempt of the
Jews. Omar took the corner of his robe, and commenced
clearing it, and all the rest followed his example."*

Further on our author proceeds: "They say that Omar,
after the conquest of Jerusalem, asked of Kaab Ebn Ishaak,
'Know you the place of the Sakrah?'—He replied, 'Towards
the wall that looks towards (qui donne au) the valley of
Gehenna, at such and such a distance.' They dug there,
and found the rock covered with dung.† 'Where do you
believe, then,' asked Omar of Kaab, ' we ought to establish a
mosque?' He answered, 'Towards the kiblah.' 'We will

---

* Fundgruben des Orients, v. p. 160.   † See also Jelal ed Deen, p. 177.

build it, then, behind the rock.' Thus the two kiblahs of Moses and the Prophet were united. 'O Ebn Ishaak,' said Omar, 'the Jews will have reason to say, This is the best of mosques!'

"According to another tradition, Kaab, having been questioned by Omar where they should build a mosque, replied, 'At the Sakrah.'—'That,' said Omar, 'is the direction of the Jews; it would be better to build it before the rock, that those who pray there may have before them the kiblah of Mecca, and not that of Jerusalem, for the Prophet has not ordered us to turn to the rock Sakrah, but towards the Caaba.'"*

There are two points in this narrative which in themselves ought to suffice to settle the question at issue. The first is, that Omar entered the Temple area by the Gate of Mohammed. That gate still exists south of the Jews' Wailing-place, 270 feet from the south-western angle of the Haram area (woodcuts Nos. 7 and 17). It is now blocked up nearly to the roof, and, except the filth, perfectly answers to the description in the text. To say that Omar entered there creeping on his hands and knees to look for a rock which "stands out erect and alone," to use the expression of Eusebius— the highest pinnacle of the surrounding localities—is simply absurd. He went to look for the foundations of Solomon's Temple. He entered by the gate nearest them, and found them within the area I have ascribed to the Temple.

The other point is what is said about water running down the steps, which, luckily, we are enabled to explain from a passage in Antoninus. He says, "Before the ruins of

---

* Fundgruben, *loc. cit.*

Solomon's Temple, under the street, water runs down to the fountain Siloam. Alongside of the portico of Solomon, in the Basilica itself, is the seat on which Pilate sat when he heard our Lord." * It may be added that the position of the cisterns and watercourses in the Haram area all justify this description if applied to the position of the Temple as restored above, but all is utterly unintelligible if referred to the Dome of the Rock.

There is only one other quotation with which I need trouble you at present. Arculfus, the French Bishop, whose account of the Holy Places is the most distinct and complete we have, tells us that "in that famous place where once the Temple was constructed with great magnificence, the Saracens have erected a square house of prayer, on the remains of some old ruins, which house may contain about 3000 persons." †

As this was written certainly eight years after the year 72 Hejira, when Abd el Malek is said to have completed the Dome of the Rock, it proves that the Saracens had not at that time broken the treaty Omar had made with the Patriarch Sophronius.

Had the Saracens erected also the Dome of the Rock at that period, it seems impossible that Arculfus could have omitted to mention it, as the chief, and by far the most important building of the two. Besides this, there is no whisper that

---

* Ante ruinas Templi Salomonis sub platea aqua decurrit ad fontem Siloam. Secus porticum Salomonis in ipsa Basilica est sedes in qua sedit Pilatus quando Dominum audivit.— Ant. Mart., ch. xxiii.

† Ceterum in illo famoso loco ubi quondam Templum magnifice constructum fuerat in vicinia muri ab oriente locatum nunc Saraceni quadrangulam orationis Domum quam subjectis tabulis et magnis trabibus super quasdam ruinarum reliquias construentes vili fabricati sunt opere ipsi frequentant quæ utique domus tria hominum simul ut fertur capere potest. Ad. Sanc. Ord. Ben., sæc. iii. pars ii. p. 524.

the treaty with Omar had at that time been broken, or even infringed upon. All that had then been done was to build the Mosque el Aksah, which stood within the precincts of the Temple, which had been assigned to the Saracens by the treaty.

Unless, indeed, we can put on one side the whole account of the Holy Places as given by Arculfus, it amounts to as absolute a proof as could well be afforded, either that the Dome of the Rock was described by him under the denomination of the Anastasis, or that it did not exist when he was at Jerusalem in the year 700.

I must not, however, weary you with long quotations from unfamiliar authors, and you must for the present be content with assertions, which I make with the perfect knowledge that nothing will be so easy as to contradict them, and refute all arguments based upon them, if I am wrong.

I am not an Arabic scholar myself, but Sir Henry Rawlinson had the kindness to place his unrivalled library at my disposal. I employed a competent scholar to abstract and translate all those passages he could find bearing on Jerusalem. I carefully examined these, and compared them with all that has been published and translated, and the result of the whole is a firm conviction in my mind that down to the age of Abd el Malek, and later, the Mahometans knew perfectly what were the limits of the Temple; that their Sakhra was in the vaults or substructures of that building; and that they neither built nor pretended to have anything to do with the building we now know as the Mosque of Omar.

Of course in the loose and rambling narratives of Oriental historians there are many passages which may be read as applying to any state of matters, and it is not always easy to distinguish between what are quotations and what assertions of the authors ; but still the general result is clear and distinct enough, and, from all I know, the impression in my mind is that the Mahometans knew perfectly what the limits of the Temple were, and that their Sakhra was covered by the Mosque el Aksah.*

There is still, however, another mode by which the accuracy of the knowledge of the position and dimensions of the Temple, possessed by the people of that age, may be tested.

If any one will take the trouble of restoring the plan of the Temple of Herod, from the description of Josephus and the Talmud, he will be able to fix the position of the centre of the altar within a very few feet either way. Having done this, if he will draw a line east and west through the altar and the Holy of Holies, he will find that it cuts the centre of the Jews' Wailing-place. Now, we know that the Jews had access to the Temple area in the time of Constantine, and, when driven forth, they naturally sought the spot nearest to the Holy Place to lament over it. They must have known then exactly where it was—and there we find them at this hour.

If, on the other hand, we draw a line north and south through the same altar, we cut the kibleh of the Aksah ; and according to the Mahometan authors recording the events of Omar's visit, we find that he ordered the kibleh to be placed behind the Sakhra, in order that those who pray there may have before them the kibleh of Mecca, and not that of Jeru-

* The bulk of the passages bearing on this subject are quoted at length in my work on the Ancient Topography of Jerusalem, p. 130 et seq.

salem : because, he added, the Prophet has not ordered us to turn to the rock Sakhra, but towards the Caaba.

It is, therefore, interesting to find the kibleh of the Aksah exactly behind the site of the Altar of the Jews, and is, amongst others, a tolerable evidence that the site of that altar was known when the mosque was built.

What Abd el Malek apparently did, was to increase the Mosque of Omar (woodcut No. 16) northward, so as to include the Sakhra, or what he supposed to be it, within its walls.*

---

* Auxit Templum ita ut petram inferret in Templi Adytum. El Macin, p. 69. The same words occur in Eutychii Annales, ii. p. 364. The expression, it may be added, is wholly devoid of meaning if applied to a circular building with the Sakhra in the centre of it. No augmentation of circle is required to include its central point.

CONCLUSION.

In the argument I have just addressed to you, I am afraid I must plead guilty to having led you by a side road, or long way round, before bringing you to the point at which I wished you finally to arrive. But if, in doing so, I have presented to you some clearer views than you before possessed of the celebrated Temples of the Jews, you will perhaps excuse the digression.

At the same time, I think you can hardly fail to see the direct bearing of the argument on the question as to who built the Dome of the Rock. I trust that the argument which I have laid before you has made it clear—1st, The Temple of Herod was a building 600 feet square, neither more nor less; 2nd, That it was situated in the south-west angle of the Haram area; 3rd, That both the Christians and the Moslems knew perfectly well, in the seventh century, what the dimensions of the Temple were, and where it was situated.

If this be so, it is perfectly certain that the Saracens knew that the Rock which now occupies the floor of the so-called Mosque of Omar was outside the sacred precincts of the Temple, and, consequently, they could not, for this reason alone, besides all the others above adduced, have enshrined it in the splendid edifice that is now the principal architectural ornament of Jerusalem.

The Temple of the Jews was a sacred spot to the Moslems, because their Prophet had started thence on his night journey to heaven, and had noticed it with honour and reverence in the Koran. They also respected it because they hoped at that time to rally the Jews under their standard, and to convert them to Mahometanism.

In consequence of this, Omar first built a mosque* within its precincts; and Abd el Malek, in the 72nd year of the Hejira, A.D. 691, completed the Mosque el Aksah within its sacred boundaries. The mosques of the Mogrebins and the Malakites were afterwards built, all within the 600 feet I have assigned to its limits. The idea of their going outside what was known to be the Temple area to build a second mosque, in direct violation of the treaty so recently concluded with the Christians, is not only most improbable in itself, but is contradicted by all we learn from both the Christian and Mahometan histories of the period.

If, then, the Dome of the Rock was not built by the Saracens, it must have been built by the Christians; there are no third parties in the field who could have done it. If this be so, I would again ask, what church did Constantine or any other Christian priest or monarch build in Jerusalem over a great rock with one cave in it, but the Church of the Holy Sepulchre?

Till a reasonable answer is given to this question the arguments of my opponents halt. And no attempt has yet been made to reply to it, or to supply its place with any satisfactory suggestion.

In conclusion, let me add that I first took up the question

---

* The real Mosque of Omar still exists adjoining the S.E. angle of the Aksah, as shown in woodcuts No. 7 and No. 16. The name, as applied to the Dome of the Rock, is simply a mistake of the Christians; by Mahometans, that building is known as Kubbet es Sakhra, or "Dome of the Rock."

on architectural grounds, which seemed to me at the time, as they do now, quite sufficient to settle it. Feeling, however, that others might not have the same implicit faith in that form of argument, I next investigated it historically. Lastly, putting both these aside, I took it up on the topographical grounds I have just been explaining to you. These are three very distinct and separate roads, but they all lead direct to the same point.

Turn it and twist it which way I would, whatever path I attempted to pursue, I have never been able to escape the conviction that the first conclusion I arrived at was the only correct one. I do not mean to assert that the question is without difficulties, the road always without ruts or roughnesses; but I do assert that, so far as I can judge, an immense preponderance of evidence, from whatever point it is viewed, is in favour of the conclusion that the building known as the Dome of the Rock at Jerusalem is the identical church which Constantine built over what he believed to be the Sepulchre of Christ.

APPENDIX.

APPENDIX A.

Extract from the Itinerary of the Bordeaux Pilgrim. Circa A.D. 333.
*From a MS. in the Library at Verona. 'Revue Archéologique,'
August,* 1864.

" Ibi etiam constat cubiculus in quo sedit (Solomon) et sapientiam
discripsit. Ipse vero cubiculus uno lapide est tectus. Sunt ibi et
scepturia magna aequae subterraneae et piscinae magno opere edifi-
catae et in aedem ipsam ubi templum fuit quem Salomon aedificavit
in marmorem ante aram sanguinem Zacchariae ibi dicas hodiae
fusum, etiam parent vestigia clavorum militum qui eum occide-
runt per totam aream ut putes in ceram fixum esse. Sunt ibi
et statuae duae Hadriani. Est et non longe de statuas lapis
pertusus ad quem veniunt Iudaei singulis annis et unguent eum
et lamentant se cum gemitu et vestimenta sua scindunt et sic
recedunt. Est ibi et domus Ezichiae regis Iudae. Item exeun-
tibus Hierusalem ut ascendas Sion in parte sinistra et deorsum
in valle iuxta murum est piscina quae dicitur Siloa, habet qua-
driporticum et alia piscina grandes foras; haec fons sex diebus
atque noctibus currit, septima vero die est sabbatum in totum
nec nocte nec die currit. In eadem ascenditur Sion et paret
ubi fuit domus Caifae sacerdotis, et columna adhuc ibi est in qua
Christum flagellis cederunt. Intus autem intra murum Sion
parit locus ubi palacium habuit David et septe synagoge quae
illic fuerant una tantum remansit relique autem arantur et
seminantur sicut Esaias propheta dixit. Inde ut eas foris murus
de Sion euntibus ad portam Napolitanam ad partem dextram
deorsum in valle sunt pariter ubi domus fuit sive praetorium
Ponti Pilati ubi dominus auditus est antequam pateretur : ad
sinistra autem parte est monticulus Golgutta ubi dominus crucifixus est. Inde quasi ad lapidem missum est cripta ubi corpus
ejus positum fuit et tercia die surrexit : ibidem modo iusso

Constantini imperatoris basilica facta est, id est dominicum, mire pulchritudinis habens ad latus excepturia unde aqua levatur et balneum a tergo ubi infantes labantur."

APPENDIX B.

Extract from an anonymous Description of the Holy Places, published by Dr. Titus Tobler, from a Codex in the British Museum. Cottonian Lib. Titus.

INCIPIT DESCRIPTIO SANCTORUM LOCORUM.

"I. SI quis ab occidentalibus partibus Jerusalem adire voluerit, solis ortum semper teneat et hierosolymitani loci oratoria ita inveniet, sicut hic notata sunt.

"II. In Jerusalem est cubiculum uno lapide coopertum, ubi Salomon sapientiæ librum scripsit, et ibi inter templum et altare in marmore ante aram sanguis Zachariæ fusus est. Inde non longe est lapis, ad quem per singulos annos Judæi veniunt et unguentes eum lamentantur et sic cum gemitu recedunt. Ibi est domus Ezechiæ, regis Juda, cui ter quinos annos ad vitam Dominus dedit. Deinde est domus Caiphæ, et columna, ad quam Christus ligatus, flagellatus, cæsus fuit. Ad portam neapolitanam est prætorium Pilati, ubi Christus a principibus sacerdotum judicatus fuit. Inde non procul est Golgotha vel Calvariæ locus, ubi Christus, filius Dei, crucifixus fuit, et primus Adam sepultus ibi fuit, et Abraham ibi Deo sacrificavit. Inde quasi magni(o) lapidis jactu versus occidentem est locus, ubi Joseph ab Arimathia Domini Jesu corpus sanctum sepelivit. Ibi est ecclesia a Constantino rege speciose fabricata. A monte Calvariæ sunt XIII pedes ad medium mundi contra occidentem; a sinistra parte est carcer, ubi Christus carceratus fuisse narratur. In dextra parte sepulchri prope est monasterium latinum in honorem sanctæ Mariæ virginis, ubi ejusdem domus fuit. In eodem monasterio est altare, ubi Maria, mater Domini, stabat, et cum ea soror ejus Maria Cleophe et Maria Magdalena flentes dolentesque, quia in cruce Dominum videntes. Ibi dixit Jesus matri suæ: MULIER, ECCE FILIUS TUUS; discipulo: ECCE MATER TUA. Ab hoc loco, quantum potest arcus bis mittere sagittam, in

orientali parte est templum Domini a Salomone factum, in quo
a justo Simeone præsentatus est Christus.   In dextra parte hujus
templi Salomon templum suum ædificavit et inter utrumque
templum porticum speciosam struxit columnis marmoreis.   In
sinistra parte est probatica piscina."

The editor's remark on this, is " Wenn nun ein kleiner theil
der beschreibung des Innominatus auf ein hohes alter vor dem
einfalle der Perser zurückschliessen lässt, so unterliegt es dem-
nach keinem zweifel, dass der andere und zwar grössere theil
hochstens im 11 jahrhundert geschrieben wurde " (p. 243).

No one familiar with the subject or the localities would
probably be found to dispute this conclusion of Dr. Titus
Tobler's.   The whole description, from the beginning down to
the words " In dextra parte sepulchri," is so nearly identical with
the narrative of the Bordeaux Pilgrim (Appendix A), as to leave
no doubt but that the two are describing the same state of things,
and about the same time.   The mention of the Templum Domini
and the Maria Latina in the latter part of the extract proves
that it could not have been written before the 12th century,
inasmuch as the name Templum Domini was first applied to
the " Dome of the Rock " by the Crusaders, and was not known
before they reconsecrated that building to Christian worship, and
the monastery of Maria Latina equally belongs to that age.

The remainder of the narrative, referring to other localities
about Jerusalem, seems also to belong to the latter date, but has
no reference to our present subject.

The point which makes this MS. valuable is the fixation of
the site of the " Porta Neapolitana."   The Prætorium of Pilate
certainly was the Turris Antonia.   At all events even those who
contend for the present tradition must admit that it was eastward of the Arch of Ecce Homo.   The Porta Neapolitana, which
was attached to it, must consequently have been one of the gates
of what is now known as the Haram Area, and the testimony of
the MS. seems equally clear that the Church of Golgotha, and
the Anastasis, were then within that sacred enclosure.   In so far
as such evidence can decide a case of this sort, it appears to be
conclusive, and ought to be considered as final.

APPENDIX C.

Inscriptions on Dome of Rock.

THE following is a copy of this inscription in the original French, as translated by the Comte de Vogüé and M. Schefer, both of whom are scholars perfectly competent to the task. The corresponding English passages will easily be found in Sale's or any other translation of the Koran.

The important passage on which they rely for a date is the following:—

" A construit cette coupole le serviteur de Dieu Abd [Allah el Imam el Mamoun], prince des croyants, l'année 72. Que Dieu l'ait pour agréable et soit content de lui. Amen."

The words between brackets De Vogüé asserts are a falsification, Al Mamoun's date being 198-218 Hegira. It is to be presumed however that those who wrote the name could read the date, and it is most strange, to say the least of it, that the proper date should not have been inserted, *if it was done during the reign and by order of that Chalif;* if done, as I suspect, during the reign of Saladin, the writers may have wished to combine as well as to obscure the two traditions.

What is important to know here is that there is a falsification in this part of the inscription; others must settle how it was introduced.

To proceed, the next passage is—

"Louange à Dieu! Il n'a pas de fils. Il ne partage pas l'empire de l'univers. Il n'a pas besoin d'aide. Publie ses grandeurs (17, 111).

" Le ciel et la terre sont son domaine; il donne la vie et la mort. Sa puissance s'étend sur toute chose (57, 2).

" O vous qui avez reçu les Écritures, ne sortez pas de la foi, ne dites de Dieu que la vérité. Jesus est le fils de Marie, l'envoyé de Dieu et son Verbe; Dieu l'a fait descendre dans Marie, il est son souffle. Croyez en Dieu et ses envoyés. Ne dites pas qu'il y a une Trinité en Dieu, cette croyance vous sera meilleure. Il est un. Gloire à lui! Comment aurait-il un fils? Tout ce qui est au ciel et sur la terre est a lui; il se suffit à lui-même (4, 169).

" La grâce de Dieu est sur ton apostolat, Jésus fils de Marie!
La paix sera sur moi au jour de ma naissance, au jour de ma
mort, et au jour de ma résurrection, a dit Jésus, vrai fils de Marie,
celui sur lequel ils élèvent des doutes. Dieu ne saurait avoir
de fils; loué soit son nom! Il parle, et ce qui n'était pas est.
Dieu est mon Seigneur et le vôtre, adorez-le; c'est le chemin du
salut" (19, 34, 37).*

APPENDIX D.

Description of the Dome of the Rock by Theodericus, A.D. 1172.

"Ipsum denique templum inferius octogonum esse manifestum
est; inferius usque ad medium spatium nobilissimo marmore
ornatum et a medio usque ad superiorem, cui tectum incumbit,
limbum musivo opere decentissime decoratum.   Ipse vero limbus,
circulariter per totum templi ambitum circumductus, hanc con-
tinet scripturam, quæ, a fronte vel ab occidentali introitu
inchoans, secundum solis circuitum sic est legenda, in fronte:
Pax æterna ab æterno patre sit huic domui; in secundo latere: *Templum Domini sanctum est. Dei cultura est.   Dei sanctificatio est;* in
tertio latere; *Hæc est domus Domini firmiter ædificata;* in quarto
latere: *In domo domini omnes dicent gloriam;* in quinto: *Benedicta
gloria Domini de loco sancto suo;* in sixto: *Beati, qui habitant in
domo tua, Domine;* in septimo: *Vere Dominus est in loco suo sancto,
et ego nesciebam;* in octavo: *Bene fundata est domus Domini super
firmam petram.* Præterea versus orientem juxta beati Jacobi
ecclesiam columna quædam musivo opere in muro depicta est,
supra quam talis est descriptio facta: *Columna romana.* Superior
autem murus angustiori circulo, fornicibus interius sustentatus,
circumducitur, qui, plumbeum gestans tectum, in summo gran-
dem pilam et super eam crucem deauratam habet stantem. Per
quatuor januas intratur et exitur, unaquæque janua suam de
quatuor mundi plagis respicientem. Subsistit autem ipsa ecclesia
quadratis fornicibus VIII, columnis XVI, cujus muri et cœlatura
musivo opere nobiliter sunt decorata. Ambitus vero chori qua-

---

* De Vogüe, 'Le Temple de Jérusalem,' p. 85.

tuor habet fornices sive pilaria et octo columnas, quæ interiorem
murum, cum ipsius testudine in altum porrecta, gestant. Super
ipsos autem chori arcus linea in circuitu circulariter porrigitur
hanc ex ordine continens scripturam *Domus mea domus orationis
vocatur, dicit Dominus. In ea omnis, qui petit, accipit, et qui quærit,
invenit, et pulsanti aperietur. Petite et accipietis, quærite et invenietis.*
In superiori vero circulo similiter circumducto hæc continetur
scriptura : *Audi, Domine, hymnum et orationem, quam servus tuus
orat coram te, Domine, ut sint oculi tui aperti et aures tuæ intentæ
super domum istam die ac nocte. Respice, Domine, de sanctuario tuo
et de excelso cœlorum habitaculo.* In introitu proinde chori altare
in honore beati Nicolai habetur ferreo pariete inclusum superius
limbum habente et hanc scripturam continente, in fronte : *Anno
millesimo C° 1°, indicta quarta, epacta XI ;* in sinistro latere : *Ab
Antiochia capta XLIIII. Jerusalem LXIII ;* in dextro latere :
Tripolis LXII. Berytus LXI. Ascalona XI anni. Verum versus
orientem ad latus chori locus ferreo pariete januas habente cir-
cumseptus omni veneratione dignus habetur, in quo Dominus
noster Jesus Christus, ad templum cum oblatione sua XL° nati-
vitatis suæ die delatus, a parentibus oblatus est, quem ad templi
ipsius introitum senex Simeon in ulnas suscepit et ad locum obla-
tionis detulit, in cujus loci fronte hi versus sunt descripti :—

" HIC FUIT OBLATUS REX REGUM VIRGINE NATUS.
    QUO LOCUS ORNATUR, QUO SANCTUS JURE VOCATUR.

Juxta eundem locum vix uno remotus cubito lapis ille situs est,
quem Jacob patriarcha supposuerat olim capiti suo, super quem
dormiens scalam ad cœlos vidit erectam, in qua descendentes et
ascendentes angelos vidit, et dixit : *Vere Dominus est in loco isto, et
ego nesciebam.* In cujus loci fronte isti continentur versus :—

" CORPORE SOPITUS, SED MENTE JACOB VIGIL INTUS
    HIC VIDIT SCALAM, TITULUM DIREXIT AD ARAM.

" Hinc per orientalem portam ad capellam beati Jacobi apos-
toli, fratris Domini, intratur, ubi idem, de templi pinna præcipi-
tatus et, fullonis fuste cerebro confracto, ab impiis Judæis
peremtus, primo in valle Josaphat templo contigua sepultus et

postea a fidelibus in eundem locum relatus honorifice, ut eum decuit, sepulturæ traditus est, super cujus sepulchrum hoc scriptum est epitaphium :

"DIC, LAPIS ET FOSSA : CUJUS SUNT, QUÆ REGIS OSSA?
SUNT JACOBI JUSTI.   JACET HIC SUB TEGMINE BUSTI.

Est autem ipsa ecclesiola rotunda, inferius latior, superius angustior, columnis VIII sustentata et picturis optime decorata.* Redeuntibus ab ipsa etiam per eandem portam, retro ostium ipsius portæ, ad sinistram quadrangulus quidam occurrit locus in lato et longo quinque habens pedes, in quo Dominus stans et ubi esset interrogatus in Jerusalem, quam in medio orbis sitam asserunt esse, respondit et hoc: Locus ille Jerusalem appellatur. Item retro idem ostium e regione prædicti loci seu versus aquilonem alius occurrit locus illas continens aquas, quas Ezechiel propheta vidit de templo a latere dextro.   Redeuntibus in ecclesiam majorem ad meridiem juxta chorum, immo sub ipso choro ostium paret, per quod gradibus fere XLV in cryptam intratur, ubi scribæ et pharisæi mulierem in adulterio deprehensam adduxerunt ad Dominum Jesum eam accusantes, cui pius magister peccata remisit et a condemnatione liberavit.   Quo exemplo pere-

---

* The chapel here described either is the Dome of the Chain, or a building which stood where it now stands. If Theodericus is as minutely correct in his description of this as he is of the larger building, it is certain that the building we now see must have been entirely remodelled by the Saracens since his day, and its appearance would certainly justify such an hypothesis. The tradition in the text, however, raises another and much more important question. Why was St. James buried here? On what possible hypothesis could such a tradition have arisen, except it was known that the Dome of the Rock was the tomb of his brother? If it had been suspected that the larger building had been erected by the Saracens, or that it covered the altar of the Jews, or even that it stood within the Temple precincts, would St. James have been buried there, or a chapel erected in his honour on that spot? If, on the contrary, it was known that the larger building was the tomb of Christ, nothing could be more natural and proper—as the text expresses it—than that his brother should have his sepulchre in juxtaposition.

The Tomb of St. James is now transferred back to the Valley of Jehoshaphat, to the rock-cut sepulchre of the family of Hezir.—De Vogüé, *Temple de Jérusalem*, p. 44.

grinis indulgentia ibidem dari solet. Habet autem ipsa ecclesia fenestras inferius XXXVI, superius XIIII, quæ simul junctæ faciunt quinquaginta, et est in honore nostræ dominæ sanctæ Mariæ consecrata, cui etiam principale altare articulatum est. *Ipsa quoque ecclesia a beata Helena regina et ejus filio Constantino imperatore fertur esse fundata.* Videamus ergo, quoties vel a quibus ipsum templum ædificatum fuerit sive destructum. Sicut legitur in libro Regum, primus rex Salomon templum Domini divina missione magnis impensis ædificavit, non rotundum, uti nunc conspicitur, sed oblongum, quod usque ad tempora Sedechiæ, regis Judæ, permansit, qui captus a Nabuchadenasor, rege Babyloniorum, in Babyloniam captivus adductus est, et cum eo Juda et Benjamin captivati similiter in terram Assyriorum translati sunt. Mox Nabuzardan, princeps coquorum ipsius, in Jerusalem cum exercitu veniens templum et civitatem ipse cremavit, et hæc prima ejusdem templi fuit eversio. Post LXX autem captivitatis annos reversi ad terram Juda filii Israel, ducibus Zorobabel et Esdra, cum favore et permissione Cyri, Persarum regis, idem templum in eodem loco reædificaverunt et, quoad melius potuerunt, ornaverunt. In reædificando autem templo et civitate una, ut fertur, manu lapides, alia propter gentilium circummanentium assiduas infestationes gladios tenebant. Hæc ergo secunda fuit templi reædificatio. Postea eadem civitas, ut in gestis Machabæorum legitur, ab Antiocho, rege Syriæ, etsi non penitus, tamen ex maxima parte vastata est, ornatus templi penitus destructus, sacrificia prohibita muri diruti et quasi in solitudinem tam civitas, quam templum redactum est. Quod postea Judas Machabæus et fratres sui cum adjutorio divino, fugato Antiocho ejusque ducibus de Judæa propulsis, reædificaverunt et renovaverunt, et reparato altari sacrificia et oblationes, sicut prius, sacerdotibus dispositis instituerunt. Hæc quoque templi tertia fuit restitutio, quæ usque ad tempora permansit Herodis, qui, ut Josephus refert, contradicentibus licet Judæis, hoc templum solo dejiciens majori et sumptuosiori opere aliud instituit. Et hæc quarta templi reædificatio fuit, quæ etiam usque ad tempora Vespasiani et Titi perduravit, qui, expugnata omni provincia, tam civitatem, quam templum fun-

ditus everterunt.   Et hæc quarta templi fuit eversio.   Post hoc,
ut paulo ante dictum est, *Hoc templum, quod nunc videtur, ad
honorem Domini nostri Jesu Christi ejusque piæ genitricis ab Helena
regina et ejus filio imperatore Constantino, constructum est.** Et hæc
etiam quinta templi fuit restitutio."—*Theoderici libellus de Locis
Sanctis, editus circa* A.D. 1172, *edited by Dr. Titus Tobler.   St. Gallen,*
1865.   Pp. 38 to 46.

APPENDIX E.

THE following are the two passages of the Talmud which refer to
waterworks under the Jewish altar, as translated by Constantine l'Empereur de Oppyck.—(*Elzevir edition of Middoth.   Leyden,*
1630.)

CHAPTER III., SECTION 2.

Cornu autem inter *Occidentem* et *Austrum* habebat duo foramina
instar duarum narium exilium : per quæ sanguis sparsus cum
super pulvinum sive fundamentum *Occidentale* tum super fundamentum *Australe* descendebat et miscebatur uterque sanguis in
canale ac effluebat in torrentem Kedron.

SECTION 3.

Inferius in pavimento ad idem cornu erat locus quadratus
unius cubiti ubi tabulæ marmoreæ annulus infixus erat qua
descendebant in foveam sive camarinam eamque purgabant.
Præterea ascensus erat ab Austro altaris 32 cubitorum cujus
latitudo 16. habebatque foramen in parte *occidentali* ubi effunde-
bant sanguinem super pulvinum *occidentalem* et pulvinum *meridio-
nalem* per quos defluens deinde miscebatur ac tandem effluebat
eo etiam projiciebant rejectanea sacrificia pro peccato ex avibus
disumpta.

---

* To this Dr. Tobler adds : "Eine
nicht minder merkwürdige stelle
findet sich im äusserste seltenen Büch-
lein des ungarischen Pilger Gabriel
aus dem 1514 (Compendiosa quedam
descriptio urbis Hierusalem die also)
lautet, Templum Sancti Sepulchri,
per S. Helenam est ædificatum in
Monte Moria ut tradunt Judæi."
The only disinterested witnesses in
the case. P. 194.

APPENDIX F.

Locality of Zion in Early Writers.

From ' Notes and Queries,' March 7, 1865.

Mr. Fergusson says (Smith's ' Dictionary of the Bible,' i. 1026),—

"It cannot be disputed that, from the time of Constantine downwards to the present day, this name (Zion) has been applied to the western hill [rather, south-western hill] on which the city of Jerusalem now stands, and in fact always stood."

As Mr. Fergusson, who makes this statement, earnestly maintains that Zion was the eastern hill, it is natural that others, including those who advocate the same opinion, should assume, from his not having stated it, that there is no evidence later than the time of Constantine for supposing Zion to be the Temple Hill; hence the point has not, it seems, been properly investigated. It will hardly be thought any want of respect to Mr. Fergusson if it be supposed that he has not the same acquaintance with early patristic writers that he has with architecture. That it has been generally applied to the south-western hill (on which part of the city stands) is certain, but in and from the time of Constantine this has not been universal.

Eusebius, in his ' Life of Constantine,' seems to make Zion the south-western hill; but he appears to do this by mystically applying the name to the side of the valley opposite to the Temple Mount. I rely on him as a witness that the hill on which the Temple had stood was then known as identical with Zion. Eusebius says (*In Esaiam* xxii.),—Σιὼν μὲν γὰρ ὅρος ἐστὶν ὑψηλόν, ἐφ᾽ οὗ ὁ νεὼς τοῦ θεοῦ ᾠκοδόμητο. (Montfaucon, *Collectio nova Patrum*, ii. 441ᵇ.)

Epiphanius, in the latte rpart of the 4th century, thus identifies Zion with the eastern hill, on which the fortress (ἄκρα) had stood (north of the Temple, on the same ridge, be it remembered). In speaking of Golgotha he says,—ἄντικρυς γάρ ἐστι τὸ τοῦ Ἐλαιῶνος ὅρος ὑψηλότερον, καὶ ἀπὸ σημείων ὀκτὼ ἡ Γαβαὼν ὑψηλοτάτη· ἀλλὰ καὶ ἡ ἄκρα ἡ ποτὲ ἐν Σιών, νῦν δὲ τμηθεῖσα, καὶ αὐτὴ ὑψηλοτέρα ὑπῆρχε τοῦ τόπου. (Epiph., *Panarium*, ed. Petavii, i. 394ᵈ, ed. Dindorf, ii. 415.) Probably for σημείων ὀκτὼ we should read σημείων πέντε (ε instead of ή): for this would be about the distance to Neby Samwil, the only place, it seems, that could be intended. It may be worth mentioning that Origen in the third century identified Zion with the Temple mountain. He says (*In Johan.*, tom. xiii. 12), οἱ δὲ Ἰουδαῖοι τὸ Σιὼν θεῖόν τι νενομικότες . . . . καὶ διὰ τοῦτο ἐν αὐτῷ ᾠκοδομῆσθαι τὸν ναὸν ὑπὸ τοῦ Σολομῶντος λέγουσι. (Ed. De la Rue, iv. 222ᵈ.)

As every locality connected with Jerusalem is so earnestly discussed, every contribution in the way of *evidence* has its value. I believe that the passage from Eusebius and that from Epiphanius have never been brought forward before on this subject; at least I do not remember to have seen them, and I noted them in the course of my own patristic studies.

Many who do not at all agree with Mr. Fergusson in his strange theory as to the site of the Holy Sepulchre being where the Mosque of Omar now stands, fully hold that the Zion of Scripture was the eastern hill, the fortress (" City of David ") occupying the northern part; amongst these I may mention the Rev. J. F. Thrupp, in his 'Antient Jerusalem,' 1855, and Mr. Lewin, in his 'Sketch of Jerusalem,' 1861.

S. P. TREGELLES.

Plymouth.

APPENDIX G.

117, *Jermyn Street*, S.W.
March, 1865.

MY DEAR SIR,

It may almost be inferred from the Scripture itself, that the site of the Crucifixion was just north of the Temple. In the Epistle to the Hebrews it is argued that the greater sin offerings, which were burned without the camp, were typical of our Saviour, who also suffered here; a resemblance which is much more meaning if we suppose the scene of the Passion to have been the Place of the Skull, marked by the remains of the victims so burnt. Nothing can be more natural than to suppose a place close outside the Temple wall set apart for the purpose.

In Ezekiel xl. we find that the sacrifices were slain and washed at the north gate, where also the priests who had charge of the altar resided.

Yours truly,

H. BRANDRETH,

Fellow of Trin. Coll., Cambridge.

APPENDIX H.

THE following answers to a string of nine objections to my views about Jerusalem, which appeared in the 'Quarterly Review' in October last, were published in the 'Athenæum' journal of the 21st January of this year. Neither the objections, nor consequently the answers, are of much importance; but it may be as well to reproduce them, as illustrations of the class of arguments that have been usually employed in this controversy. It is always perfectly easy to answer them, but unfortunately hardly ever possible to do so in such a form that the objection and the answer shall reach the same class of readers.

Mr. Lewin, for instance, in his 'Sketch of Jerusalem,' p. 146 *et seq.*, publishes a list of thirteen similar objections. It would be as easy to give a categorical reply to each and all of them, as to those of the Quarterly Reviewer. But where? and, after all, *cui bono?* Not one of these objections touches the real points at issue, nor are they such as would be put forward by any one who grasped the true scope and significance of the argument. It is hardly worth while wasting one's strength in skirmishing with the outposts, while the two armies are lying opposite one another in battle array, awaiting the real issue which must decide the victory.

Assertion 1, p. 404.—"Nothing is historically more certain than that the Church of the Resurrection was again and again burnt down and destroyed by the Moslems."

Answer.—El Hakem did burn and destroy the Basilica of Constantine, sometimes called the Church of the Holy Sepulchre, and no trace of it is left, except in the Golden Gateway; but there is absolutely no hint in any author, Christian or Mahometan, that I know of, that the Moslems either burnt or destroyed the Anastasis or Tomb of Christ. To have done so would have been considered nearly as great a sacrilege by the Mahometans as by the Christians. Hence its preservation to this day.

Ass. 2.—"For this Basilica and chapel of Golgotha Mr. Fergusson's imagination is alone responsible."

Ans.—The Basilica is minutely described by Eusebius (Vita Constantini, iii. 25 *et seq.*). Arculfus describes the "Golgothana Ecclesia" as "pergrandis Ecclesia orientem versus" (Act. Sanct., sæc. iii., par. ii., p. 546), as we learn from Antoninus (ch. xix.), 400 feet distant from the Anastasis. The "quatuor Ecclesiæ" are mentioned three separate times by the monk Bernhard (Act. Sanct., sæc. iii., p. 524), by Eutychus (ii. 219). Plans are given and special descriptions of the four by Arculfus (*loco cit.*).

Ass. 3.—" We do not believe there could have been a burying-place not more than 200 feet north of the great gates of the Temple."

Ans.—There was no external gate of the Temple on the north, and Josephus says (Bel. J., V. vii. 3), " While John and his faction defended themselves from the tower of Antonia and from the northern cloister of the Temple, and fought the Romans before the tomb of Alexander," &c. It is, therefore, certain that there were tombs at the spot indicated, which is also confirmed by Ezekiel xliii. 8, 9, and Nehemiah iii. 16.

Ass. 4.—" The cave under the Sakrah was not a sepulchre. Dr. Pierotti has proved it was a cesspool."

Ans.—Dr. Pierotti has not established his right to be quoted as an authority on this or any other question. It would be easy to prove the untenableness of this filthy hypothesis, but the conditions under which I write force me to refrain from argument.

Ass. 5.—" Solomon and Herod would not have cooped up" (on the top of a hill!) " the Temple into a corner where there was barely room for it to stand."

K

Ans.—Reasons are given in the Bible why David chose the threshing-floor of Araunah for the site of the Temple. The building erected by Solomon, with its appurtenances, covered exactly one-eighth of the area of the Temple afterwards erected on the same spot by Herod. If there was room for the larger, *à fortiori* there was abundance of space for the smaller, and that determined the site.

Ass. 6.—" A deep fosse strengthened the northern fortifications of Antonia and the Temple."

Ans.—I obtained, through the Editor, the reference to this. It is Bel. J., I. vii. 3. In this passage Josephus was speaking of the Temple of Zerubbabel before the Antonia or that of Herod was commenced. The last-named king doubled the extent of the Temple (Bel. J., I. xxi. 1), when the fosse was necessarily filled up and included within the precincts. The reviewer, consequently, is quoting a passage which refers to a state of affairs which had ceased to exist long before the siege of Titus.

Ass. 7.—" The Jews fought the Romans at Bezetha, from Antonia and the Northern Cloister of the Temple."

Ans.—The reference to this I also obtained through the Editor. It is Bel. J., V. vii. 3. The word Bezetha does not occur in the passage, nor is there the remotest allusion to it. It is a mere misquotation of the reviewer, like the previous one.

Ass. 8.—" The Bordeaux Pilgrim, A.D. 333, in proceeding towards the Nablous Gate, had the church on his left hand," &c.

Ans.—There is no authority for his assumption that the Porta Neapolitana was the Damascus Gate. It seems more probable that it was the gate of the "New City." Till this is settled, no argument can be based upon it.

Ass. 9.—" Mr. Fergusson is the *sole* authority for the marvellous transmigration of the Sepulchre from Moriah " (who placed it there ?) " to the present site ! "

Ans.—Gibbon, in a note to Chapter LIX. of his History, says, " The clergy artfully confounded the Mosch or Church of the Temple with the Holy Sepulchre, and their wilful error has deceived both Vertot and Muratori."

APPENDIX I.

The Temple of Herod and the Sepulchre of Christ.

From ‘ The Reader,’ 8th April, 1865.

Sir,—My attention has been called to your admirable report of
Mr. Fergusson's late Lecture; and it has revived the deep interest
I feel, in common with every thinking man, in the Temple of
Herod and the Sepulchre of Christ. I join the two, for to my
mind they are inseparable, and with your permission I will tell
you how.

I am not unacquainted with the mediæval and modern literature of those holy places; but, after all, I felt obliged to go
back for satisfaction to the original records in Greek of Josephus,
Eusebius, and Socrates. Of Mr. Fergusson I have no personal
knowledge whatever, but I gladly offer my independent testimony, such as it is, to the truth of his views. I believe that
from those authors alone it can be proved that the so-called
Mosque of Omar stands over the spot of the Sepulchre, and the
Mosque el-Aksa on the site of the Temple.

To take the Temple first. Josephus has so repeatedly asserted
that the Temple of Herod was four-square, and that each side
was a stadium, or 600 feet, from out to out, that no words need
be wasted on that point. Now, the Haram within which it stood
is very extensive, being not 600 feet square, but oblong, about
1520 feet along the east wall, and something more along the
west; and about 930 feet along the south wall, and something
more along the north. For reasons which will be seen by and
bye, the Temple *could not* have stood in the centre of this large
Haram, or in either of its angles but that of the south-west; for,
besides the reasons which will be seen hereafter, there only is
the Jews' Place of Wailing at the stones of the Temple—there,
evidently, was the bridge leading from the king's palace to the
royal cloisters of the Temple—and there, lastly, on two sides of
the angle, the allotted 600 feet of the Temple are clearly defined.

In what follows I have tried in vain to vary to any good

K 2

purpose the account I have already given in the appendix to
' What I saw in Syria, Palestine, and Greece; so that, if you
think proper, I will reproduce it here with a few additional
remarks.

Before I proceed, however, I had better guard your classical
readers against the errors of Valesius in his commentary on
Eusebius. One will be sufficient to show his character. The
new church at Jerusalem, built by Helena at the expense of
Constantine, and so attributed to either, was called "The New
Jerusalem," says Eusebius. Helena named it "New Jerusalem,"
says Socrates. That is quite a mistake, says Valesius; for what
is meant is, that Helena, having first built the new city of
Jerusalem opposite the old city, went and did so and so (p. 228
of his notes on Eusebius).

I now go on to observe that, when Herod built the Temple on
the site of the former one, he walled in at the same time a space
of ground adjoining it of equal dimensions altogether with the
Temple itself : τὸν ναὸν ἐπεσκεύασε, καὶ τὴν περὶ αὐτὸν ἀνετειχίσατο
χώραν τῆς οὔσης διπλασίαν. (Josephus, Bell. i. 21, 1.)

He also built a fortress for the Temple, and called it Antonia.
It stood, says Josephus, at the north-western corner of the
Temple area, and communicated with the cloisters of the Temple
by means of staircases; Ἡ δὲ Ἀντωνία κατὰ γωνίαν δύο στοῶν ἔκειτο
τοῦ πρώτου ἱεροῦ, τῆς πρὸς ἑσπέραν καὶ τῆς πρὸς ἄρκτον, κ. τ. λ. (Bell.
v. 5, 8.)

The shape of Antonia must have been long and narrow : long
from south to north, and narrow from east to west : for mention
is made of Titus casting a mound during the siege against that
part of the north cloister wall—κατὰ τὴν βόρειον στοάν—(Bell. vi.
7)—which the fortress did not touch.

The area of Antonia with its cloisters was about half that of
the Temple, and ran the whole length of the remainder of the
western wall of the Haram, terminating at its north-west angle.
Its cloisters, being 500 ft. long, and—with the intervening court
—200 ft. broad, made up the circuit of cloisters allotted by
Josephus (Bell. v. 5, 2); for he says—speaking of the Temple
cloisters as well—πᾶς κύκλος αὐτῶν εἰς ἓξ σταδίους συνεμετρεῖτο,

περιλαμβανομένης καὶ τῆς Ἀντωνίας.　The remainder of the allotted
area, being about 420 ft. long by 200 broad, was occupied by the
Fortress itself.

So that here, in the entire area of the fortress Antonia, is
about one half of the additional space of 360,000 square feet (the
space occupied by the Temple) enclosed by Herod; and the other
half—with a fraction over—lay between the east side of the
Temple and the wall.

It is thus clear that, A.D. 33, the Holy Rock stood in the
country, at some little distance outside the fortress Antonia, and
the wall of the Temple, with its dyke, to the north of the latter.
It stood on a space of ground entirely open to the country, with
no obstructions whatever beyond the ordinary enclosures of
gardens and cemeteries in the suburbs of a city. And so it continued till ten or eleven years after the Crucifixion. Then it was
that Agrippa did such great things by extending the walls of
Jerusalem. For the population had increased to overflowing;
and houses had begun to creep up the hill to the north of the
Temple, beyond the circle of the ramparts, and so were quite
naked and exposed. In order, therefore, to protect them, he
built a new wall enclosing the hill Bezetha. This wall made a
sharp angle at the north, and, running in a direct line to the
dyke of the north wall of the Temple (called the Kedron dyke,
from its opening eastward to the brook Kedron), it there joined
the old wall of Herod to the east of the Temple: τῷ ἀρχαίῳ περι-
βόλῳ συναπτὸν εἰς τὴν Κεδρῶνα καλουμένην φάραγγα κατέληγεν.

Τοῦτο τῇ προσκτισθείσῃ πόλει περιέθηκεν Ἀγρίππας, ἥπερ ἦν πᾶσα
γυμνή. (Bell. v. 4, 2.) Not only so. The fortress Antonia, as we
have seen, ran along the west wall of the Haram to its north-west
angle, and there terminated. In order to separate the fortress
from the hill Bezetha and its new town, Agrippa dug a deep
trench (which doubtless extended to the new wall at the east),
and thus greatly increased the height and security of Antonia.

So Bezetha was designedly cut off from Antonia ὀρύγματι βαθεῖ·
διεταφρεύθη γὰρ ἐπιτηδὲς ὡς μὴ τῷ λόφῳ συναπτόντες οἱ θεμέλιοι τῆς
Ἀντωνίας εὐπρόσιτοί τε εἶεν καὶ ἧττον ὑψηλοί. διὸ δὴ καὶ πλεῖστον
ὕψος τοῖς πύργοις προσεδίδου τὸ βάθος τοῦ τάφρου. (Bell. v. 4, 2.)

But all this took place *eleven years after the Crucifixion*, when, with the exception of those unprotected houses which had begun to creep up the hill, the whole country to the north and north-east of the Temple was open and exposed : ἥπερ ἦν πᾶσα γυμνή.

There, then, in a garden outside the city and Temple walls altogether, stood the Holy Rock by itself. It did not stand as it does now, with flights of steeps around it leading up with archi-tectural effect to any building placed over it, and then with other steps leading down of necessity to the cave within it. We will suppose the steps taken away altogether, and the Rock standing out by itself, with an easy access to the cave, on the level plat-form of the garden. We will suppose, further, within a stone's throw of it, a small rounded hill in the shape of a skull, and the public pathway of the city running near it. We will go still further, and assume for the present that that little hill is Gol-gotha, and the cave of that rock the Sepulchre of Christ.

Thus consecrated by the most momentous event that ever occurred, what became of this Rock, with its Sepulchre of Christ, after that ? For three hundred years the whole city, with its suburbs, was in the hands of the heathen, who besieged it, and burnt it, and levelled it, walls, towers, Temple and all, with the dust ; and then rebuilt it, and called it by another name. And the very name of Jerusalem was long forgotten, and the actual spot of the Sepulchre of Christ was for ages blotted out from the knowledge of man.

Upon this point the language of the early historians is too plain to admit a doubt. In the fourth century, when Constan-tine and his mother Helena had become Christian, she had a dream which impelled her to go to Jerusalem. " And she searched diligently," says Socrates, " for the sepulchre in which Christ was buried and out of which He arose, and with great difficulty, and by God's help, finds it :" καὶ δυσχερῶς μὲν, σὺν Θεῷ δὲ εὑρίσκει. The difficulty was briefly this : Seeing that they who regarded the things of Christ honoured His Sepulchre after His death, they who abhorred the things of Christ covered the spot with mounds of earth, and built over it a temple to Venus, and set up her image, in order to do away the memory of the spot altogether; and up to the time of Helena's visit the design was successful:' μη ποιουντες μνημην του τόπου· τουτο μεν ουν παλαι τρουχώρει. (Socrates, *Eccl. Hist.* i. xvii.)

And so speaks Eusebius of the long success of their infamous scheme: τῶν ἀθέων καὶ δυσσεβῶν ἀνδρῶν τα κατα της ἀληθείας μηχανήματα μακροις παρετείνετο χρόνοις. (Eusebius, *Vit. Const.* iii. 26.)

The truth is that the undissembled design of heathendom, with intervals of contemptuous toleration, was, by means such as this, utterly to root out even the name of Christianity from the earth. They persecuted and tortured and slew its resolute believers, and threw down its churches, and burned every copy of the Scriptures that could be found. (Eusebius, *Eccl. Hist.* viii. 2.) Had they succeeded in this last most deep and Satanic object, all, humanly speaking, would have been over. But God in His mercy willed otherwise; and Constantine became Christian, and hidden copies of the Scriptures came forth, and churches were rebuilt, and the Sepulchre of Christ, the author of our faith, was brought to light. Nor was that all. It matters not which of the royal house, mother or son, built that church over the Holy Rock. The New Jerusalem was built *face to face* with the celebrated one of old:' ἡ νέα κατεσκευάζετο Ἰερουσαλὴμ, ἀντιπρόσωπος τῇ πάλαι βοωμένῃ. (Eusebius, *Vit. Const.* iii. 33.)

And so Socrates: "On the very spot of the Sepulchre the Emperor's mother built a magnificent house of prayer, and called it New Jerusalem, having made it *face to face* with that desolate old one." οἶκον μὲν εὐκτήριον ἐν τῷ τοῦ μνήματος τόπῳ πολυτελῆ κατεσκεύασεν Ἰερουσαλήμ τε νέαν ἐπωνόμασεν, ἀντιπρόσωπον τῇ παλαιῇ ἐκείνῃ καὶ καταλελειμμένῃ ποιήσασα. (Socrates, *Eccl. Hist.* i. 17.)

The church thus built was called " New Jerusalem," a symbol of the Church of Christ; the Temple of Herod, " Old Jerusalem," a symbol of the Church of the Jews.

The conclusion to me was irresistible. When I stood, as I did, by the Holy Rock in the Haram, looking south, I stood on the site of the Church of Constantine, *face to face* with the site of the Temple of Herod.

Your obedient servant,

S. SMITH.

Lois Weedon Vicarage,
April 4, 1865.

APPENDIX J.

The Mosque at Hebron.

During my recent excursion in Palestine I visited the Mosque at Hebron, and had an opportunity of examining that long-closed sanctuary with more care than has been permitted to any one in modern times. A brief description of it may therefore be considered as an appropriate appendix to this account of the Temple and Holy Sepulchre at Jerusalem.

The conditions under which I obtained admission to the mosque are detailed at some length in a letter I wrote to the 'Times' on my return, and which was published in that journal on the 28th November last. The circumstances were amusing enough, and in some respects very gratifying, but hardly of such a nature as to justify a record beyond the columns of the Ephemeridæ, and need not, therefore, be repeated here. One remark on them is nevertheless requisite in order to explain the sequel. However pleasing a "state and festival" occasion of this sort may be, it is singularly unfavourable to calm investigation or to careful examination of the details of any building. During the whole time I was in the mosque I was surrounded by a *magna caterva*, consisting of all the magnates of the place civil and military, and all the priests and servants attached to the mosque. All these showed the greatest desire to be civil to me, and to point out everything important in their eyes, though these frequently were not the objects which appeared the most so to me. I, on the other hand, was nervously anxious to do nothing which might hurt their feelings or offend their prejudices, and I never could quite make up my mind how far I might go, nor how long a time I might be allowed to stay.

Under these circumstances it will be perfectly understood that the plan and section now submitted are mere sketches, and do not pretend to any merit, except to being better than any others hitherto published. Indeed I cannot but feel that, putting them forward now, I am exposing myself to a "frightful exposure" from any traveller who, with more leisure and better opportunities, is enabled to make a really correct plan of the building, and to examine it with the requisite care. I have, however, no sympathy with those who, from fear of a little personal inconvenience, shrink from publishing such knowledge as they possess, after having taken every available means of satisfying themselves of the correctness of their investigations. All this plan pretends to be is that it is better than its predecessor. No one will rejoice more than I shall, when it is superseded.

The principal result of my examination was that I ascertained with certainty that there was nothing inside the enclosure older than the time of the Crusades. The Gothic building which occupies the whole of the southern end was certainly erected either in the last half of the 12th or first half of the 13th century. The Saracenic buildings are all subsequent to this, and there remains nothing now which can be ascribed to the Byzantine or any earlier period.

The most disappointing result was that I could not discover any means of access to the cave below, except through the small circular hole in the floor. Nor can I now feel sure whether any such exists at the present day, though my personal conviction is that none is now to be found.

The circumstances under which Abraham, more than 3600 years ago, purchased the cave of Machpelah from Ephron the Hittite are so minutely recorded in the 23rd chapter of Genesis, and are so familiar to every one, that they need not be repeated here. It is the oldest record we possess of any such transaction, and there does not seem a shadow of a reason for doubting that it took place precisely as recorded; and as little for not believing but that the cave now enclosed in the Haram area at Hebron is the identical sepulchre so purchased, and in which the bodies of the patriarchs and their wives were afterwards buried.

From the time of the transaction described in the Book of Genesis till after the Christian era, we lose all sight of these remarkable sepulchres. Neither in the Bible nor in any profane author is there the slightest allusion to them, so that we are left to conjecture the state in which they may have been when the present enclosure was erected. Judging from analogy, we may assume that they were left untouched and unadorned, guarded only by the respect of the descendants of the patriarchs for the memory of those buried within them.

From what we know of the modes of burial among the Jews, and such indications as we afterwards receive, we gather that the patriarchs were laid in *loculi* cut in the sides of a natural cave, the body being protected by a stone, closing the mouth or side of the *loculus*, in which it was laid. There is no reason for supposing that any special precautions were taken to preserve the bodies from decay. They were probably wrapped, as was usual, in a winding-sheet, and placed in the grave without a coffin, though it may be with spices which would prevent the smell from being offensive during the first period of decay.

If such were the case, a few years would suffice to dissolve their bodies into the original dust. In a century or two no trace of them would be found. And consequently, when the cave was enclosed within the splendid wall that now surrounds it, it was in honour of the memory, not of the bodies of the patriarchs, that it was erected.

The only exception to this might be the body of Jacob, which was embalmed in Egypt, and might consequently be expected to last as long as those we now find in that country ; but it is more than doubtful if the best-preserved Egyptian mummy would last one thousand years in an open natural cavern in the moist and variable climate of Palestine. Long before the Christian era he too must have become an undistinguishable heap of dust.

It is now fabled that Joseph rests here also, but we know that his mummy was deposited at Sichem, and the burial of this patriarch here rests wholly on a later tradition. According to an older one, Adam was buried at Hebron. A later one required that Adam should be buried under the cross at Golgotha, and Joseph seems then to have taken his place here, a tradition which the Saracens seem blindly to have adopted.

The first author who mentions these sepulchres after the

writer of Genesis is Josephus. His account is painfully short
and unsatisfactory. All he says is, " It is said that Abraham,
the progenitor of the Jews, inhabited this city (Hebron), after
he migrated from Mesopotamia, and from it went to Egypt with
his children. Their monuments ($\mu\nu\eta\mu\epsilon\iota\alpha$) are to be seen in this
city at the present day, made of beautiful marble and carved in
the most elegant manner." (B. J., IV. ix. 7.)

What Josephus here refers to are evidently cenotaphs in the
form of marble sarcophagi , and as the introduction of these stone
coffins into Judæa was certainly due to the Romans, we may
guess pretty nearly what their form was. But the curious part
of the narrative is that there is no hint of the existence of the
stone enclosure. No one can suppose that it was erected after the
siege of Jerusalem by Titus : it consequently must have existed
in his day ; and it is by no means clear why so careful a chronicler of the architectural doings of his countrymen should omit
all mention of one of the most remarkable buildings they ever
erected.

Still less is there any reason to suppose it was erected by
Solomon, to whom tradition as a matter of course ascribes it, or
to any of the earlier Jewish kings. The Temple which Solomon
built at Jerusalem, of which the Jews boasted so much, was
insignificant, as compared with this, as an architectural pro-
duction, and no early writing or tradition ascribes the Hebron
enclosure to him or to them.

Though the result only of negative evidence, what little we
learn from history would lead us to believe that the external
wall belongs to the great building epoch of Herod ; and a com-
parison with what we find in Jerusalem and elsewhere, which
certainly belongs to that age, confirms this deduction in every
particular.

The substructions of the Temple at Jerusalem, especially on
the west side, at the Jews' Wailing-place, are identical with this
in all their masonic forms ; and there are near the Holy Sepulchre
some remains which are of the same age as the Wailing-place,
but which have also the offsets and buttresses which characterize
this specimen. The stone at Hebron is better and harder than

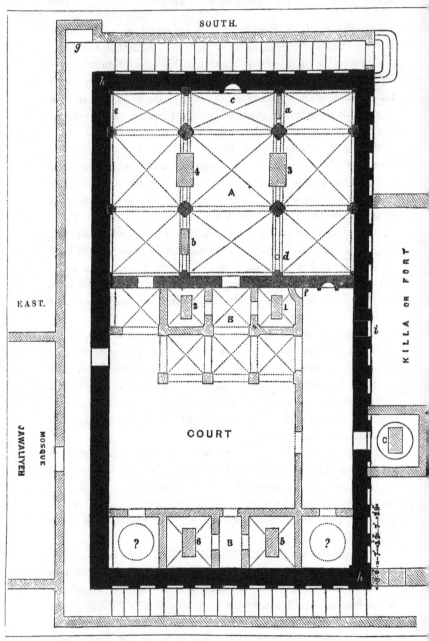

SOUTH.

EAST.

KILLA OR FORT

MOSQUE   JAWALIYEH

COURT

[No. 29.]   Plan of the Mosque at Hebron. From a Sketch by the Author.*

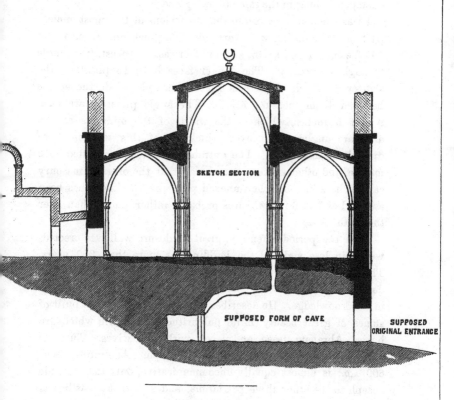

REFERENCES.

A. Gothic Building.
B B, Porches, A.D. 1331.
  C. Tomb of Joseph, A.D. 1393.
  a. Pulpit.
  b. Merhala.
  c. Mihrab.
  d. Aperture leading to Cave.
  e. Greek Inscription.
  f. Print of Mahomet's Foot.
  g. Fountain.
h h. Minarets.
   i. Supposed position of original Entrance.

1. Shrine of Abraham.
2. Shrine of Sarah.
3. Shrine of Isaac.
4. Shrine of Rebekah.
5. Shrine of Jacob.
6. Shrine of Leah.

     Jewish Buildings.
     Gothic Buildings.
     Mahometan Buildings.

* I am indebted for the woodcut to the courtesy of the Editor of the 'Builder.' It was engraved for that Journal, and published on the 24th of December last.

at Jerusalem, which gives it a fresher and newer look; but on the whole there seems no reason for doubting that these several examples belong to the same building epoch.

I was enabled to ascertain the dimensions of this most ancient part of the building with very tolerable precision. It measures 198 feet north and south, and 112 feet east and west, from angle to angle externally. The longer faces have 16 pilasters, the shorter 8. Each of these is 3 feet 9 in. wide, while the spaces between them measure 7 feet. The angle pilasters are each 9 feet 6 inches, which is the width of the minarets at the alternate angles. The exact thickness of this wall is more difficult to determine. The entrance doorway is revetted with marble, and otherwise so encumbered that the original masonry cannot be seen. In the annexed plan the thickness has been assumed at 7 ft. 6 in., which is probably rather under than over the truth.

After the period when this great enclosure wall was erected, we again lose sight of the building for more than 300 years. The next mention we have of it is in the Itinerary of the Bordeaux Pilgrim, A.D. 333, and what he says does not add much to our knowledge. He describes the square enclosure as built of stones of great beauty (miræ pulchritudinis), within which are buried Abraham, Isaac, and Jacob, with their wives. There is no mention there of either Adam or Joseph. Antoninus, about 600 A.D., is almost equally uncommunicative, only that he adds Joseph to the other three patriarchs, and says that a basilica is built there "in quadriporticus," whatever that may mean, with an atrium uncovered in the centre. At that time the enclosure seems to have been divided by a railing in the centre, one side appropriated to the Christians, the other to the Jews, who at that period seem to have had equal access to the graves of their forefathers.

The most detailed account we have in that age is by Arculfus, about the year 700 A.D. In his day Adam was the fourth patriarch, but he was not buried inside the cave, but outside, in the earth, "because the Lord had said, Dust thou art, and shalt to dust return." In consequence of this "he was not laid in a stone

sepulchre cut in the rock " (non in saxeo in petra exciso sepulchro
super terram ut ceteri de semine ejus honorati quiescunt, sed in
terra humatus terra tectus); from which we gather that the
three others were placed in loculi cut in the sides of the cave,
though how arranged it is extremely difficult to understand.

If the cenotaphs now on the floor of the church at all represent
the arrangements below, the patriarchs were buried at the outer
edge of the cave, their wives towards the inside, unless indeed
the cave was entered from the north; but this supposition is
contradicted by the geological formation of the rock, in so far
as we can at present judge. Each of the graves, Arculfus informs
us, had a tombstone or cenotaph placed over it of the size of
the grave, but wrought into the form of a shrine (quasi ad formam
alicujus Basilicæ parvas memorias fabricatas). These probably
were the marble monuments which Josephus describes; but
whether they were in the cave or on a floor above it, as they are
now, is by no means clear.

The sepulchre of Adam at that time seems to have been that
now said to be occupied by the bones of Joseph. When the
Christians repossessed Jerusalem they interpreted literally the
tradition that the cross stood over the grave of Adam; so it
became necessary to transfer his sepulchre to that locality. The
tradition was then renewed of Joseph having been buried here,
though the Bible certainly would lead us to believe that his
mummy rests at Sichem.

The historians of the time of the Crusades add very little to
our knowledge of this sanctuary. Indeed it is more than doubtful whether the two principal authorities, Sæwulf in 1102 and
Benjamin of Tudela in 1163, ever visited the locality, and did not
describe it merely from hearsay. The former certainly blunders
when he first makes Adam rise from the dead in consequence
of the blood of Christ which fell on him from the cross, and then
buries him at Hebron, though there he only describes the graves
of the three, Abraham, Isaac, and Jacob, with their wives, and
mentions the sepulchre of Joseph where we now find it, outside
the Haram. We may therefore doubt whether he saw " each of
the three monuments like a great church, with two sarcophagi in

each, one for the man and one for the woman." What we learn from Benjamin was that Abraham had already been canonized under the title of St. Abraham, and we know that a very few years afterwards (1167) Hebron was erected into a see under that title.

Since its recovery by the Saracens, 1187, the entrance to the sanctuary has been practically closed to the outside world; and so far as our knowledge extends, the cave itself has never been accessible even to the true believers. It is at least quite certain that no Mahometan author, and they are tolerably numerous, pretends to have visited it himself, though many of them report at secondhand the stories of those who assert that they have been more fortunate. Jelal ed Deen,* for instance, relates how one Abu Bekr, having presented 4000 dinars to the mosque, claimed permission to enter. The priests put him off month after month, till the winter set in and the snows closed the roads, when consequently there were no pilgrims or strangers about. They then took him to a spot between the tombs of Abraham and Isaac—where the present opening is—and raised the pavement, when he descended seventy-two steps with a man named Saluk, &c. In the cave he saw the patriarchs lying in the flesh on their tombs, with splendid beards; and tells of other wonders, which make it certain he either never descended, or invented what he is reported to have seen.

The story told in Quatremère's 'Histoire des Sultans Mamlouks de Makrisi,' vol. ii. p. 239, is more to the purpose. It is there related that, a poor idiot having fallen through the hole that now exists in the floor, a servant of the neighbourhood descended and rescued him. He relates also how several eunuchs descended the same way into the cave, though they brought back very little satisfactory information.† These and various other passages seem to make it clear that no other entrance than the opening in the floor is known to exist in modern times;

---

* Translated by Reynolds, p. 361.
† The story told by Makrisi is confirmed in every particular by Mejr ed Deen as translated by Von Hammer, 'Fundgruben des Orients,' vol. ii. 376.

whether the priests have any other means of access is not known. If they have, they have hitherto kept it a profound secret, not only from Christians, but from their co-religionists.

There is one other passage in Jelal ed Deen (p. 359) which it may be worth while quoting, as showing what was the belief of educated Moslems on this subject in the 15th century. " Abraham," he says, " was buried over against Sarah ; Isaac was buried there over against Rebekah ; Jacob was buried at the gate of the Tomb Cavern ; Leah over against Jacob. Then the sons of Jacob and Esau with his brethren met together, saying, Let us keep the doors of the cave open, and bury therein whosoever dieth amongst us. Some dissension ensuing, one of the brethren of Esau was enraged and killed one of the sons of Jacob. Then the others struck Esau, and knocked off his head in the cave. They carried away his trunk and buried it without the head, leaving the head in the cave. This they then closely blocked up, and put tombstones inscribed, ' This is the tomb of Abraham,' &c. Then they closed up the entrance. All those that came thereto went round the spot and missed it, so that no one could find it till the Greeks came. They opened the gate, and, entering, built a church. Afterwards, God giving victory to Islam, the Moslems seized all the sacred buildings and destroyed the church."

If this means anything, it would lead us to believe that the entrance was then at the north, between the tombs of Jacob and Leah, which is the impression obtained, as above stated, from the disposition of the graves. But on the whole it seems more probable that those who placed the cenotaphs on the floor of the mosque, where we now find them, had no knowledge of the disposition of the tombs below. Perhaps there are no means of ascertaining it, or it may be, that, like mediævalists in general, they were utterly careless on the subject.

What we do learn from the Mahometan historians—especially Makrisi and Mejr ed Deen—is, that the buildings round the courtyard containing the cenotaphs of Abraham and Sarah, as well as those of Jacob and Leah, were erected (A.H. 732), A.D. 1331, by Sultan Mohammed ibn Kalaon, and the tomb of Joseph by the Emir Jaghmuri, A.D. 1393—all the Mahometan buildings in the enclosure falling within the limits of the 14th century.

All this, however, throws no light on what is the most interesting architectural problem connected with this mosque, after the determination of the age of the Herodian enclosing wall. No history or description which has yet been cited gives any hint as to the erection of the Gothic building which occupies the whole of the southern end of the Haram. When I first saw it, I jumped to the conclusion, a little too hastily perhaps, that it belonged to the early part of the 13th century. Judging from the progress and form of that style in Italy and the south of France, where that peculiar variety of it alone is found, I was no doubt correct, and, on looking over the data, am inclined to believe I placed it rather too early than too late. It has been pointed out, however, that the Crusaders never obtained possession of Hebron after the end of the first Latin kingdom of Jerusalem (1187). We are therefore forced to adopt one of two hypotheses,—either that the development of the style was so much more rapid in the East than in the West as to admit of its being squeezed into the twenty years during which the bishopric of St. Abraham lasted (1167-87); or to assume that it was erected by a Christian architect for the Mahometans after the time of Saladin.

Judging from what took place at Constantinople some three centuries afterwards, there is no *a priori* improbability in the last supposition. The mosques erected there are purely Byzantine in form and detail, and were erected by Christian architects for their new masters. The same may have happened here; besides that the mosque is in many respects unlike a church. It has no choir or apse; its orientation—about which in Palestine they were particular in those days—is wrong; and there are other points about it which can scarcely be made to tally with the idea of its having been originally designed for Christian worship.

On the other hand, De Vogue's researches ('Eglises de la Terre Sainte') do show an early development of the style, which, if his later dates are to be depended upon, would render not very improbable the supposition that it might belong to the latter half of the 12th century. If it does, we must admit that we borrowed not only the pointed arch, but the Pointed style, from the East, to a greater extent than we have hitherto been willing to allow. Pending further information on the subject, I confess I feel inclined to adopt the assertion of Jelal ed Deen above quoted, and to believe that the Mahometans destroyed the church of the Christians, and erected this building perhaps out of its ruins.

Much of the interest that would attach itself to the date of this building is lost from the circumstance of its insignificance in an architectural point of view; and had it been found anywhere else, it would scarcely have attracted any notice. Even now, it is more with reference to the progress of Pointed architecture in the East than as regards the Tomb of Abraham that it is desirable that the question should be somehow settled.

Its dimensions are not considerable : it measures only 70 feet from the entrance door to the mihrab, and this space is divided into three very unequal pier arches — the first 25 feet from centre to centre of the columns ; the next 30 ; and the last to the south only 15. In the other direction it measures about 95 feet — the side aisles being 30, the central 35 feet in width. The four pillars are clustered; the one at least that I drew, consisting of twelve shafts. These support a flat rib stretching across from wall to wall, as usual in Italian Gothic ; and between them is the usual intersecting vault, which in the centre aisle admits of a clerestory range of windows, amply sufficient to light the interior in that climate —almost more, indeed, than is required at present, as the whole has been carefully whitewashed, and so repeatedly as to obliterate the more delicate mouldings, whose character might serve to fix the date. To the height of about six feet the walls all round are wainscoted with marble slabs of Saracenic design, and placed there, Makrisi tells us, in 1331.*

---

* See also ‘Fundgruben,’ *loc. sup. cit.*

The tombs—or more properly the cenotaphs—of the patriarchs, which are now shown, are built up of stone in the usual form of those found in the regal mausolea at Constantinople and elsewhere. They are covered with vails of rich silk embroidered in gold, in very elaborate and beautiful designs, and which entirely hide the structure they cover. The name of the person in whose honour the cenotaph was raised is embroidered in the centre of each. A similar cenotaph exists at Jerusalem in honour of David, in the church on Sion called the Cœnaculum. Its coverings are richer and more elaborate than those at Hebron, but of the same general character and design.

The tombs of Abraham and Sarah, as well as of Jacob and Leah, are each in small apartments by themselves, outside the mosque. The places of honour are reserved for Isaac and Rebekah, who occupy prominent positions in the centre of the mosque, under elaborate canopies, either of marble or of painted wood—I failed to ascertain which—and certainly look far more important than any of the others, though why this should be so is difficult to explain.

Under the pier arch, between the tombs of Abraham and Isaac, is an opening in the floor, circular in form, and about eighteen inches in diameter. This is shown as the only opening or means of access to the cave below; and taking into consideration all I heard on the spot, all that history tells us, and all the circumstances of the case, I am inclined to believe it is so. Still, this is just one of those points on which a traveller situated as I was, may be misled. I can only say, I looked everywhere, and saw no trace of any other opening, and no credible witness has recorded his knowledge of any other since the time of the Crusades.

The impression left on my mind was, that originally there must have been an entrance to the cave from the exterior, in the centre of the west wall, where shown on the plan, and I requested the Rev. Mr. Barclay, of Jerusalem, if he had an opportunity, to try and verify this conjecture. I heard from him a few days ago. In a letter dated 23rd February he states, "That the greater part of the wall in the Killa is so encumbered with

buildings, that it is impossible to make any satisfactory examination of the great bevelled stones; nor will this be possible,"
he adds, "till the time comes when it may be effected by the
removal of the masonry, &c." This he looks upon as possible,
"as the feeling of fanaticism seems to have lessened very much
in Hebron. One of the Sheiks accompanied me into the Killa,
and boys brought me lights without any objections being made."

If, however, the above historical indications are to be relied
upon, it is at the north end, and not in the western front, that
the entrance should be looked for.

Notwithstanding this, the geological indications of the lay of
the strata are so distinct, that the balance of evidence seems to
indicate that the original entrance to the cave was somewhere
near where indicated on the plan.

Among the minor objects of interest connected with the
mosque, the most beautiful is the pulpit, which stands on the
right of the Mihrab against the south wall. According to a
Cufic inscription* on the border of the stairs, it was completed
A.H. 484 (A.D. 1091), for a mosque at Askalon, but brought here
by Saladin after the recovery of the place by the Moslems. As
a specimen of wood-carving, it surpasses anything I ever saw of
its class. There is a pulpit in the Aksah at Jerusalem, about
eighty years more modern than this one, and, though still good,
inferior in many respects to this. The specimens of carving
most like it, that I am acquainted with, are the celebrated gates
prepared for the tomb of Mahmoud of Guznee, which are of the
same age and style, but the patterns are larger and bolder.
Every part of this pulpit is carved and ornamented, and with
a variety of detail and exquisiteness of finish which surpass all
the other examples of that age which have yet been brought to
light.

----

* It would be extremely interesting
if the form of these Cufic characters
could be compared with those of the
inscriptions in the Dome of the Rock
at Jerusalem, given above, as copied
by De Vogüé, in Appendix C. It is a
subject on which I speak with the
utmost diffidence, but they seemed to
me nearly identical.

A Greek inscription was pointed out to me—said to be Hebrew!
—built into the wall. It was carefully whitewashed and difficult
to decipher, and did not look as if it contained any interesting
information or dates, so I did not waste any time upon it, and
am now glad that I did not, as I find that a copy of it was
obtained by Mr. Schultz, the Prussian consul, and given by him
to Lieut. Newbold, who published it in the 'Journal of the
Royal Geographical Society' (vol. xvi. p. 337). It may not be
quite correctly copied, and some of the names are probably
misspelt, but this is of very little consequence, as it merely
contains an invocation to St. Abraham to bless and protect
certain individuals at whose expense the inscription was
engraved. It probably is of the age of Justinian or thereabouts.
Close by it is an Arabic inscription, likewise built into the
wall. What it contains no one seemed to know. Is it the
inscription quoted by Jelal ed Deen, p. 361? It scarcely can
contain any historical information, or it would have been
deciphered long ago, and given to the world.

The history of the Cave of Machpelah, in so far as I am able
to make it out, seems therefore to be nearly as follows:—

The cave seems to have been left open, protected only by its
own sanctity, like so many other sepulchres in Judæa, till about
the time of the Christian era.

During the great Herodian period of prosperity and architectural magnificence, the present Haram wall was built, enclosing—not only the cave—but the rock in which it was excavated.
To this period also, in all probability, belong the sepulchres and
cenotaphs of white stone or marble mentioned by Josephus.

It seems probable that a church was erected within the enclosure about the time of Justinian, and then that other shrines
were placed on the upper level, over those which remained
below. If so, it was at this period that the doorway at the
back, by which access is now obtained, was broken through.

Nothing of these buildings now remains. The oldest erection
now standing—within the enclosure—is the Gothic building at
the south end. This certainly was not erected before 1167, nor

later than 1262—most probably, more nearly approaching the former than the latter period.

The Moslem buildings surrounding the Court all belong to the 14th century.

Since then, nothing has been added but whitewash and red paint.

I may add, that my impression is, that there is no access to the cave from the level of the floor of the mosque, except by the small aperture, about eighteen inches across, between the tombs of Abraham and Isaac. But this evidence is necessarily only negative. I saw no opening, and was told it did not exist. But the mats on the floor may have concealed it, and the priests may knowingly have deceived me.

If looked at from a merely architectural point of view, the result is on the whole, it must be confessed, somewhat disappointing, but every particular must be of interest which concerns one of the oldest burial-places regarding which we have any authentic contemporary record, and regarding whose inmates we have such a homefelt interest as all feel towards the earliest patriarchs of the Jewish race.

LONDON : PRINTED BY W. CLOWES AND SONS, STAMFORD-STREET, AND CHARING-CROSS.

Printed in the United States
By Bookmasters